INDIA IN RUSSIAN LITERATURE

INDIA
IN RUSSIAN LITERATURE

R. H. STACY

MOTILAL BANARSIDASS
Delhi Varanasi Patna Madras

Head Office: Bungalow Road, Delhi 110 007
Branches: Chowk, Varanasi 221 001
Ashok Rajpath, Patna 800 004
6 Appar Swamy Koil Street, Mylapore,
Madras 600 004

First Edition : Delhi, 1985
ISBN: 0–89581–759–4

Printed in India by Shantilal Jain at Shri Jainendra Press, A-45 Naraina, Phase I, New Delhi 110 028 and published by Narendra Prakash Jain for Motilal Banarsidass, Delhi 110 007.

PREFACE

Such facts, for instance, that references to India, accounts of travels in India, and narratives of ultimately Indian origin appear quite early in Russian literature and that motifs drawn from Hindu mythology and allusions to India occur quite frequently in Russian poetry, suggest that further study of such matters may be of some interest to both literary scholars and amateurs of Russian literature. A number of similar studies are already available dealing with the Indian background in several major literatures—e.g., Robert Sencourt's *India in English Literature* (1923); A. L. Willson's *The Mythical Image: The Ideal of India in German Romanticism* (1964); and B. Bissoondoyal's *India in French Literature* (1967). (I might also mention here Shasta Bryant's article, "The Spanish Image of India", and Keith Hitchins' "Reflections of India in Rumanian Popular Literature".*) England, with its long history of commercial connections with the Orient and, especially, with its close and rather lengthy affiliations with India within the Empire, afforded Sencourt many and varied examples of Indian influence on English literature. There was a similar relationship between France and India (Pondicherry), though on a smaller scale. In the case of Germany, with no colonial establishment on the subcontinent, the many references to and images of India in its romantic literature are largely a commentary on Friedrich Schlegel's remark that *im Orient müssen wir das höchste Romantische suchen.*

So far as Russia is concerned, her literature reflects both those periods of actual contact and intercourse with various oriental cultures so familiar to students of Russian history as well as that markedly romantic interest in Asia that is so noticeable a feature of German literature. Though we can recall many famous names out of the Anglo-Indian past (Robert Clive, William Jones), and though the achievements of German and French orientology are

*Both in *Images of India* (New York: Humanities Press, 1971). *The Image of India in Western Creative Writing* (Dharwar: Karnatak University, 1970), a collection of essays by Indian scholars, is concerned chiefly with British authors.

significant, it is only Russia that can make the claim, for example, that it was in fact a Russian (G. S. Lebedev) who is considered the founder of modern Bengali drama.

Furthermore, there are a number of interesting facts and associations, that might easily induce one to look more closely into certain relationships between various aspects of the Indic and Slavic—more specifically Russian—cultures. These cover a wide range, from such elementary things as the fact that both the Russian language and Sanskrit belong to the so-called *satem* group of Indo-European languages—more particularly, that certain Russian words (especially in their spoken oblique forms) reveal close Sanskrit affinities (e.g., the plural of the Russian word for "fire", *ogon*, *ogni*—pronounced *agni*—and the name of the Hindu god Agni) and that, as Indo-Europeanists point out, both Russian and Sanskrit share, within the IE family, certain specific and striking similarities, to such matters as the effective use the poet Nikolaj Gumilev, for example, makes of a Hindu motif when he writes:

> I have lost thee as once
> The frenzied Nala his Damayanti lost.

We might also mention here Afanasij Nikitin's account of his travels in India in the fifteenth century, Count Sergej Uvarov's remarkable enthusiasm for Indian studies, Aleksandr Ostrovskij's translation of Jacolliot's French version of the Tamil play *Devadāsī*, the correspondence between Tolstoj and Gandhi, the extensive passages in the Vicomte de Vogüé's *Le roman russe* comparing the Russian and Indian characters, and Bal'mont's translation and adaptation of Kālidāsa's play, *Śakuntalā*.

My purpose, then, in writing this book has been threefold: to bring together in one study the otherwise scattered data on the various instances of contact between India and Russian literature; to trace and explain certain exemplary allusions to Indian matter in Russian prose and poetry; and to indicate, mainly through examples, the ways in which Russian writers, from the earliest times to the present, have utilized in their works either information concerning India, or themes and concepts drawn from various areas of the Indian traditions. Though my principal concern in this study has been for literary and linguistic matters, I have felt free to refer from time to time, not only to the other arts but also to certain details of both Indian and Russian history, as well as to other Indo-Russian connections of one kind or another.

The interests that resulted in the writing of this book are very likely a reflection or one small facet of a generally renewed interest in the Orient which at the present time, and for quite obvious reasons, is becoming more and more apparent in the West. This renascence of studies, both popular and specialized, monographic and multi-tomed, was heralded by Raymond Schwab's *La Renaissance orientale* (Paris, 1950) and is represented today, for example, by the recent publication of the second volume of Donald Lach's *Asia in the Making of Europe* (University of Chicago Press, 1977).

R. H. STACY

Syracuse, N. Y.

CONTENTS

CHAPTER I

INTRODUCTION

1

Prior to the Macedonian invasion of India led by Alexander the Great in 326 B.C. the knowledge of India extant in the West, i.e., among the Greeks, was minimal and extremely vague.[1] There were ancient myths about the god Dionysus' "campaign" in Asia (whence his cult in Greece had in fact come) and his conquest of India. It was this legend that inspired Alexander to follow his divine predecessor's footsteps into Asia. Herodotus (4.44) mentions the name of the logographer, Scylax of Caryanda, whom the Persian king, Darius I Hystaspis, sent on a mission to explore the Indus valley in the sixth century B.C. and who perhaps wrote an account (now lost except for a tiny fragment in Athenaeus) of his journey. This Scylax has been confused with the author of a later, fourth-century work (excerpts from which may be found in Tzetzes, the Byzantine scholar) containing those fantastic accounts of the fabulous inhabitants of India which became commonplaces in subsequent references—e.g., the Otoliknoi (people who slept in their shovel-size ears) and the Skiapodes (the "shadow-feet" who in the hot sun could lie in the shade of their own feet).[2]

Hecataeus of Miletus, the Greek chronicler and geographer, wrote c. 500 B.C. a "Voyage Around the World" (*Periodos gēs* or *Periēgēsis*), based in part on his own extensive voyages, a work that was drawn upon by Herodotus and of which brief fragments remain. In these Hecataeus, who makes the first known reference to India in Greek prose literature, mentions several Indian names, such as Caspapyros, possibly the Caspatyros of Herodotus (3.102) which has been equated with Kashmir (called Caspeiria by Ptolemy). Herodotus, perhaps the most familiar source of ancient references to India (he tells us, for instance, about the diversity of the population, the heat and cold of the Punjab, the wild cotton, and the vegetarianism of the Hindus), also mentions Caspatyros in connection with one of his most interesting tales, that of the "gold-digging ants".[3] These ants, as well as "ant-gold", are referred to later by other commentators: thus a fragment of Dion Chrysostom (first century A.D.) tells us that the ants used to mine gold were "larger than foxes but in other respects like the ants of our country". That this story was not wholly a fabrication on the part of the Greeks or Persians is shown by the fact that "ant-gold" (*pipīlika*) was known to the ancient Indians (it is mentioned in the *Mahābhārata*). It appears that both the word and the story arose from a confusion of the Mongolian words for a tribe and for "ant".[4]

Meanwhile in Aeschylus' earliest extant play, *The Suppliant Women* (c. 491 B.C.), we have the first reference to India (in this case, to Indian women) in Greek verse-drama (lines 284-286) :

> And I have heard of wandering Indian women,
> Dwelling in a land near Ethiopia, who,
> Pillion-borne, ride on steed-like camels.

On the Indian side, the first references to the Greeks ("Yavanas", derived from the Persian for "Ionians"[5]) in extant Sanskrit writings occur in Pāṇini, the famous grammarian, and in Kātyāyana, a commentator on Pāṇini. Pāṇini's dates are in doubt but he probably lived and wrote about a century before Alexander, while Kātyāyana flourished about a century and a half after Pāṇini. The fact that Pāṇini makes grammatical references to the word *yavana*, and that Kātyāyana refers to Greek script (*yavanānī*, *yavanāllipyām*) indicates that the Greeks as well as Greek documents and coins, were known at least to scholars in northern India by the beginning of the fourth century B.C. But we must remember that, beginning quite early (i.e., in the sixth century B.C.), Greek mercenaries had served in various parts of the Persian Empire, including Gāndhāra and the Indus valley. (Indeed, there were Greeks in India for just about a thousand years, from the sixth century B.C. to the fifth century A.D.) Many of these Greeks eventually settled, as did Roman soldiers at a later period in their *canabae*, where they had served. Furthermore, politically troublesome Greeks within the Persian realm were regularly exiled to what has been called the "Siberia of the Persian Empire"—Bactria.[6]

Ctesias of Cnidus (fl. 400 B.C.) was the first Greek to devote an entire treatise to India: this was his *Indika* which has come down to us only in fragments and in an abridgement by the Byzantine scholar and Patriarch of Constantinople, Photius. Ctesias spent seventeen years in Persia as court physician, first to Darius II and then to the latter's successor, Artaxerxes Memnon. Though Ctesias had ample opportunity, it seems, to supplement and correct the information already available to his Greek predecessors by listening to the accounts of Persian officials who had visited India and, possibly, by interviewing native visitors from India, what we actually have in the fragments of his *Indika* is a congeries of quaint tales of wonder and absurd exaggerations and fabrications. These absurdities added to the now considerable body of such material concerning India which for centuries continued to grow and to be told and retold.

This picture of India largely as a realm of fable was not transformed in any radical fashion in the years following Alexander's campaign in Asia. The West's knowledge, such as it was, of the geography and ethnography of northern India and contiguous regions was to a considerable extent, however, enlarged and supplemented, while various influences, operating in both directions, began to manifest themselves in some areas of the Greek and Indian cultures. Thus there seems little doubt that in the philosophy of the Sceptic school founded by Pyrrho of Elis (c. 365-275 B.C.), who accompanied Alexander to India, we can see the influence of Indic—specifically Jaina—thought[7]. In India the consequences of the Greco-Macedonian invasion were more significant: these were in fact "wide and lasting, and they had a profound effect not only on India's relations with the Western world but also on the nature of Indian civilization itself".[8] To a great extent these consequences stemmed from the impact made by the activities of and influences exerted by the Euthydemid dynasty of Bactria (c. 260-30 B.C.), an Hellenistic successor-state whose importance, however, is often overshadowed by the four others—the Seleucids, Ptolemies, Antigonids, and Attalids. It is not the purpose of this study to investigate in any detail Greek influences in India; suffice it to say that the fascinating history of the Euthydemids in Bactria and India (though knowledge is lacking in a number of areas) has been set forth in many relatively recent studies, including the classic scholarly exposition to be found in Tarn's *The Greeks in Bactria and India*.[9] Two aspects of Bactrian culture and influence must at least be mentioned here, however: the so-called Gāndhāra Buddhist art and the Bactrian coins, the latter being for their beauty "unrivalled in the whole of the antique world".[10] Unfortunately, nothing is known, either from the Greek or Indian sources, of any native Bactrian literature.

Although the actual accounts of men who accompanied Alexander and who wrote on India—the admiral Nearchus, the historians Onesicritus and Aristobulus—have been lost, some of the contents have been preserved in excerpts and citations in later writers such as Strabo and Arrian. Of special interest in these accounts are the reports—more or less accurate in this case—concerning the *Brachmans*, or Brāhmans, and the *gymnosophistai*, or "naked sages". Continued references to these, along with accounts of their ascetic practices (later associated with the popular term "fakir", a word of Arabic and not Sanskrit origin), appear down through the ages as commonplaces in European narratives, based either on fact or fantasy, concerning India. In Russia, for example, amongst the earliest references to India there is mention of the "Rakhmans" (*Rakhmane*, i.e. *Brachmanes*) in the Laurentian Chronicle of 1377.

Another *Indika* was written by an Ionian Greek, Megasthenes, who served between the years 302 and 291 as ambassador of the Seleucid king, Seleucus Nicator, at the court of an Indian king, whom the Greeks called Sandracottos, at Pāṭaliputra (Patna). It was not until the eighteenth century that this Sandracottos was correctly equated (by the French Jesuit, Joseph de Guignes, in 1772) with the founder of the Mauryan dynasty, Candragupta. Megasthenes' *Indika* is lost but considerable portions have been preserved in quotations by a long list of subsequent historians. Although discounted by Strabo and Pliny for his apparent credulity, Megasthenes seems actually to have provided the most detailed account of India up to his time, and later discoveries have frequently corroborated him on many points. Megasthenes knew of peninsular India, tells us of the class (or caste)[11] system prevailing in Magadha in the third century B.C., supplies further information on the Brāhmans, mentions Buddha, refers again to "ant-gold", and describes a governmental system remarkably like the one set forth in the *Arthaśāstra*, the Sanskrit treatise ascribed to Cāṇakya, Candragupta's minister. He even reports that prostitutes were enlisted in Candragupta's "secret service".

But he was certainly in error in stating that slavery and famines were unknown.

After the rise of the Mauryan dynasty (especially under the renowned Buddhist King Aśoka) and its decline early in the second century B.C., the Bactrian Greeks—who, according to another ancient authority, Apollodorus, eventually conquered more nations than Alexander himself—moved as far east into Central Asia as Ferghana, the present-day Kirghiz Soviet Republic, and the borders of Sinkiang. In the south, i.e., in India proper, they held "part of the North-West Frontier, the Punjab with southern Kashmir, much of the United Provinces* with a small slice of Bihar, Sind, Cutch, Kathiawar, and the northern part of Gujerat, with apparently some extension into Rajputana*".[12] They founded the port of Barygaza (Broach) on the Gujerat coast and it is noteworthy that, some sixteen centuries later, the Russian traveller Afanasij Nikitin visited the nearby and later port of Cambay after a voyage by sea from Muscat.[13] The later Bactrian kings issued bilingual coins in India: thus there is a tetradrachm of Demetrius II with the legend " of the invincible King Demetrius" in both Greek and Prakrit.

2

On the tradition founded by the logographers, historians, and other Greek writers so far mentioned (especially Megasthenes), "reinforced in the 5th century A.D. by Dionysius Periegetes and by Nonus who affected Shelley, Europe depended till the time of Cosmas Indicopleustes in the 6th century and to a large extent till Marco Polo".[14] The Romans, although the Empire at times maintained a trade with India, actually added little to the tradition, their historians and scholars serving mainly as intermediaries and commentators on their Greek predecessors. We might mention in passing, however, that such references to India that we find in Virgil's *Aeneid* (the subject is Augustus Caesar) as *...super et Garamantas et Indos/proferet imperium* (4.794-795) or in a negative comparison with Italy in the *Georgics* as

> Sed neque Medorum silvae, ditissima terra,
> nec pulcher Ganges atque auro turbidus Hermus

*These names have since been changed to Uttar Pradesh and Rajasthan respectively—Publisher.

laudibus Italiae certent, non Bactra neque Indi
totaque turiferis Panchaia pinguis harenis

(2.136-139) are significant in establishing what Curtius calls the "India topos".[15] We might also mention the name of Bardesanes (called the "Babylonian" by Porphyry) who lived in the second century of the Christian era and who may be identical with Bardesanes of Edessa. Bardesanes appears to have written a work on the *gymnosophistai* and *Brachmanes*, based on conversations with visiting Indians, of which a considerable segment is preserved in the fourth book of Porphyry's *De esu carnium*; he is also quoted in other writers, such as Johannes Stobaeus. Bardesanes describes, for instance, in quite recognizable fashion the androgynous Śiva (i.e., Śiva as *Ardhanārīśvara*) of the rock temples of Maratha.

The Roman Empire in the West ended A.D. 476. The Eastern or Byzantine Empire, however, lasted much longer—until 1453; and it was in this Eastern Empire that Cosmas Indicopleustes, mentioned above by Sencourt, lived and wrote. Although in the next section we shall return to the Middle Ages in the West, here we shall mention a number of Byzantine names and works connected, in one way or another, with India and with Indian themes. Such names and works are of special interest in view of the close cultural, religious, and literary affiliations between Byzantium and medieval Russia. But, as we shall see in Chapter II, there were very likely—in some cases, certainly—Greek originals, now lost, of some of the early Russian tales.

As for Cosmas, surnamed Indicopleustes, he was born in Alexandria and travelled as a merchant through the Red Sea and the Indian Ocean, visiting Arabia and East Africa. He later became a monk in the Sinai and, about 548, wrote the *Christian Topography* (*Christianikē topographia*), his principal object being to prove that the earth was flat and not spherical. In point of fact, the name Indicopleustes is a misnomer, since, on the basis of modern textual studies, he does not seem actually to have reached India and his statements concerning India appear to be based on the reports of others.[16] The *Topography* provides the first evidence of Christian activity in India, since the author states (again at second hand) that there were churches in Kerala and Ceylon; but the priests were Persians and it seems clear that these were Nestorians. The author also copied at Adulis in Ethiopia some inscriptions which he incorporated into his account and he thus provides us with the only record we have of the expedition into Asia made by Ptolemy Euergetes in 247 B.C. Aside, of course, from his theological concerns, the descriptions that Cosmas gives of the ports, commerce, and animals of India were deemed reliable and were depended upon for centuries by geographers and travellers. Cosmas refers again to the "Indian philosophers" or *Brachmanes*—a consistent item in accounts of India—and has also heard of China, which he calls Tzinista (from the Persian *Chinistān*).

It was another monk, John (who may be the renowned St. John Damascene), of the monastery of St. Sabas in Palestine who, during the first half of the eighth century, produced a didactic religious romance or novel entitled *Barlaam and Josaphat*.[17] This appears to be a radically Christianized version or adaptation of a work of ultimately Indian origin that reached the Greek-speaking world via Persian translations as early as the sixth century. Although the Indian original has never been found, certain features of the work suggest that it had its origin, at least in part, in a Pali *jātaka*-tale. These *jātakas* (there are over 500 of them) make up part of the Pali canon, fixed in the first century B.C., of the *Tipiṭaka* or "Three Baskets" and consist of secular folk-tales and other stories that have been "sanctified", so to speak, by being either associated with the nativity (*jātaka*) of the Buddha, or ascribed to him.

The story may be outlined as follows: an Indian king, Abenner, learns through astrology that his son, Ioasaph, will be converted to Christianity and tries to prevent this by isolating the boy in a rich palace; but Ioasaph still manages to see the sick, the blind, and the dead; he is eventually converted by the ascetic, Barlaam, and in turn converts his father and becomes a hermit. The romance has had a rich *Nachleben*, having been translated into Latin and then passing into almost all the literatures of Europe. The text of *Barlaam and Josaphat* contains many familiar fables or parables (apologues), one of the best known being "The Story of the Three Caskets" (used by Shakespeare in *The Merchant of Venice*).

The Byzantine animal fable, *Stephanites and Ichnilates*, derives from an Indian work of the fifth century (later reworked and incorporated into the *Pañcatantra* and the *Hitopadeśa*); the Indian version was translated into Persian in the sixth century and the Persian into Arabic in the eighth century. In the Arabic version, known as *Kalila and Dimna*, the authorship was ascribed to Bidpai (Pilpay)—hence the "Fables of Pilpay". The story was then communicated to various peoples who came into contact with the Arabs and Arabic literature. The Byzantine Greek translation, made by Symeon Seth in 1080, was the source of the earliest Slavic versions.[18] A Latin version and a Spanish (*Calila e Dimna*) appeared in the thirteenth century and thereafter there was an extremely wide and rapid proliferation of further translations and adaptations.

The large body of material which we call the "Alexander Romance" (familiar, along with the other "matters", in western medieval romance) derives essentially from a third-century accumulation of various factual and fanciful accounts of the exploits of Alexander the Great in India and other parts of the Orient. This compilation, known as the "pseudo-Callisthenes", was the nucleus for still further accretions, adaptations, and modifications. A Latin translation was made by Julius Valerius early in the fourth century and another by Archbishop Leo in the tenth century. By the fifth century the Alexander Romance had been interwoven with Christian themes and it was from such a Byzantine version that the earliest Slavic translations were made, beginning in the eleventh century.[19]

The story of Prester John (John the Presbyter), a Christian priest and king who was supposed to have reigned over a fabulous realm in India in the twelfth century, turns up in several literatures.[20] One version of the story contains an account of a sort of giant "panopticon", by means of which King John could survey his entire dominion and even detect distant conspiracies (*semper aliquid novi ex India*!). In Byzantium the "Story of the Indian Kingdom" seems to have served as a political pamphlet or didactic utopian tale (in the form of a letter from John) directed against the Emperor Manuel Comnenus and contrasting the situation in the Empire with an ideal Christian state. The Byzantine Greek version was translated into Latin in Dalmatia and thence, in the late twelfth or early thirteenth century, into Slavonic.[21]

In the twelfth century Michael Andreopulos translated the *Syntipas the Philosopher*, another prose remance, from the Syriac. The Syriac version was a translation from an Arabic text (now lost, but Masʻudi tells us that the *Kitāb as-Sindbād* derived from India); the Arabic derived from a Pahlevi version, and the latter in turn is believed to have been translated from an original Indian work which has never been found. The Syntipas of the title is Sindbad (*not* the sailor), this name being an Arabized version of the Sanskrit *Siddhapati* ("the perfected one"). From the Syriac version Hebrew and Persian as well as Arabic and Turkish translations were made. From these were derived many other translations and adaptations, which reached western Europe in the thirteenth century and thereafter (e.g., the Spanish *Libro de los Engannos* and the English *Seven Sages of Rome*).

There seems once to have existed a Byzantine Greek version of the apocryphal story known in early Russian literature as the "Tale of Solomon and Kitovras". The word *kitovras* is very probably a corruption of the Greek *kentauros/kentavros*, i.e., "centaur"; but this in turn may be a hobson-jobson of the Sanskrit word *gandharva* (the Gandharvas were the singers and musicians of the gods in Hindu mythology). There are a number of versions of this story, including that in the Talmud and Jewish folklore concerning Solomon and Shamir (or Solomon and Asmodeus). Nor is there any Greek text extent of the Slavic version (13/14th century) of the "Tale of the (Twelve) Dreams of King Shakhaisha". But the academician A.S. Orlov and others consider this either of ultimately Indian origin or as showing Indian (in this case, Buddhist) coloration.

The story of "Poor Leo" (*Ptōcholeōn*), which exists in several Byzantine recensions, is also very likely of Indian origin. It was this romance which served as a model for Gautier d'Arras' poem *Héraclès* in the twelfth century, and which was adapted in German and Russian versions. The latter appear in the *stariny* (or *byliny*) concerning Ivan the Merchant's Son.

3

Although the first direct translation of a Sanskrit work into a European language occurred in the seventeenth century (see below), it was in the medieval period that the *Pañcatantra* appeared in the West via Pahlevi (Middle Persian), Syriac, and Arabic translations. The *Pañcatantra* ("Five Books"), the nucleus of which dates from between 100 and 500 A.D., was originally a collection of fables, stories, and maxims designed for the instruction of princes in *nīti*, or the proper conduct of affairs. The Sanskrit work exists in a large number of versions in India, varying in length and language, the best known being the *Hitopadeśa* ("Salutary Instruction").[22] In the thirteenth century Hebrew and Spanish versions of the *Pañcatantra* were produced, these being attributed to a Rabbi Joel. From the Hebrew text John of Capua did a Latin translation c. 1270 (the *editio princeps* dates from 1480). A German version by Anton von Pforr appeared in 1483, and an Italian version by A.F. Doni in 1552. Using Doni's Italian version, Sir Thomas North did an English translation, published in London in 1570. A French translation by David Sahid was done somewhat later (1644). As noted above, material included in the *Pañcatantra* reached Russia via a Byzantine Greek version (*Stephanites and Ichnilates*); at a later period there were translations into Russian of the "western" version and, still later, direct translations were made of the *Pañcatantra* from Sanskrit into Russian.[23]

We must go back briefly, however, to an earlier age—the ninth century. Although Alcuin at the court of Charlemagne is the first Englishman to mention India, according to the *Anglo-Saxon Chronicle* King Alfred, in fulfilment of a vow, sent an envoy to India in 884 with gifts for the tomb of St. Thomas. (According to the apocryphal *Acts of Thomas*, St. Thomas the Apostle brought the gospel to India after the Crucifixion; his tomb is believed to lie in the cathedral at Mailapur, a suburb of Madras.[24]) William of Malmesbury gives the envoy's name as Bishop Sigelinus, who brought back jewels and spices from a local Indian prince. And, so far as literature is concerned, at a still earlier period Fortunatus in the sixth century continues the "India topos": King Chilperic's and St. Martin's fame has reached both India and Thule.

With the actual travels and subsequently published accounts of Marco Polo (c. 1254-1324) we reach an imporatant milestone in the history of East-West relations. Though he is more often mentioned in connection with China, Marco Polo visited southern India (including the tomb of St. Thomas) on his return journey from the Mongol court of China (he had earlier been on the Volga and in southern Russia). He tells us rather little, however, about the customs—not to mention the literature—of the people, being more concerned, merchant that he was, with such things as diamonds and rubies and the wealth of India.

But he does mention *satī* (suttee) and makes the almost standard reference to the near-nakedness of the Indians.[25] The allusions to the rubies and diamonds in Marco Polo as well as the many accounts, real, at second hand, and imaginary, of the fabulous wealth of India and its exotic inhabitants that we encounter from early Greco-Roman times down to the present day are part of the "India the Rich" tradition which becomes a commonplace in the later literatures of Europe, including Russia. Robert Sencourt, commenting on a poem by Heine which speaks of the lotus, violets, and gazelles of India, remarks appropriately: "Rubies, lotus and violets (except in a European's garden) are as rare on the Ganges as rubies and lotus would be on the Humber. Most of these literary references enter as little into Oriental feelings as a Strand divan brings back the spirit of the East".[26]

The literature of travel, both real and imaginary, was extremely popular in the Middle Ages (this was not quite so true, however, of medieval Russia).[27] Marco Polo's travels were authentic, but those of, for example, "Sir John Mandeville" were for the most part not and the name itself has become synonymous with "tall story". The *Travels* attributed to Mandeville, written originally in French and translated later into English, were published between 1357 and 1371 and soon gained enormous popularity as classics of travel literature. But they were actually the work of a Liége physician, Jehan de Bourgogne, who might have visited Egypt and Syria but who certainly excerpted the details concerning other lands, including Russia, India, and the Kingdom of Prester John, from the works of others (e.g., Odorico di Pordenone, Jacques de Vitry, Vincent of Beauvais).

It is difficult to say with exactness how many Europeans reached India in the fifteenth century; we know, however, of at least three who left accounts of their travels. Nicolo de Conti, a Venetian (fl. 1419-1444), tells us about *satī*, various other religious rites, and the Brāhmans; he visited "Bizenegalia" (Vijayanagar), the tomb of St. Thomas, and Calcutta, and departed India at Cambay. Upon his return home, de Conti related his adventures to Poggio Bracciolini, the secretary to Pope Eugene IV, and these were written up in Latin and introduced in the fourth book of Poggio's *De varietate fortunae*. In 1466 a merchant of Tver', Afanasij Nikitin, left his native city, reached India, and spent three years there. On his return journey he died before reaching Tver' and his travel accounts were left in unrevised notebook form: this is the *Khozhenie za tri morja* ("A Journey Across Three Seas") which will be discussed in the following chapter. A Genoese, Hieronimo di

Santo Stefano, visited Calcutta near the end of the century but he saw little of India beyond the coasts and his account is of little value.

The voyages of Vasco da Gama and especially his landing at Calcutta in May of 1498 mark another milestone in Indo-European relations; and, with the arrival of the Portuguese, followed by the Dutch, English, and French traders and missionaries, Europe's knowledge of India expanded rapidly and considerably.[28] The Portuguese, whose history in India is not a pretty one, established a veritable commercial empire which flourished during the sixteenth century; but although they were the last of the colonial powers to leave India (1761), their impact on Indian culture was negligible.

If we overlook the ninth-century embassy recorded in the *Anglo-Saxon Chronicle* (mentioned above), the first Englishman to visit India whom we have knowledge of—and one of the first Europeans to devote serious study to the languages of India—was a Jesuit priest, Thomas Stevens. Stevens, who came to Goa in 1579, learned Marathi and Sanskrit and published a Konkani grammar as well as a poem, *Kristana Purana*, a story of the Bible designed for Indian converts. He also noticed, some time before William Jones did so in a more thorough manner, an affinity between Sanskrit and both Latin and Greek.

A very important name in the following century is that of the Dutch minister and scholar, Abraham Roger (Rogerius). He came to Pulikat, the Dutch settlement in India, in 1630 and spent some ten years on the Coromandel coast. He died shortly after his return to Holland in 1647 and in 1651 his widow published in Amsterdam *De Open-Deure tot het Verborgen Heydendom* "The Open Door to Hidden Heathendom") which was soon translated into German and French. Here Roger describes in detail and on the basis of information from informants, the customs and religion of the Brāhmaṇas. He is the first European to mention the Vedas and he includes the first direct translation (in this instance, a paraphrase) by a European of a piece of Sanskrit literature—some of the verses of the seventh-century poet Bhartṛhari.[29]

The French are also well represented in the seventeenth century by François Bernier and Jean-Baptiste Tavernier. Bernier visited India in 1656 and remained there twelve years, observing the Mughal court of Aurangzeb where he served as a court physician.

Bernier was a precursor of the *philosophes* and tried to find a rational basis for such things as Brahmanic vegetarianism and ablutions. He viewed the Indian socio-political system through the eyes of a mercantilist and decried the absence of private property, attributing to this the principal cause of despotism. Tavernier, a jewel merchant (who, according to Voltaire, "parle plus aux marchands qu'aux philosophes"), first visited India, including the diamond mines of Golconda, in about 1641. His *Six Voyages* (1676) indicates that he probably saw more of India than any other traveler in that century.

In 1675 the Russians tried to establish diplomatic relations with Aurangzeb and the Mughal Empire: Tsar' Aleksej Mikhajlovich sent a Kazan' tatar, Muhammad-Yusuf Kasimov, to the Mughal court but the overtures were rejected. Later, towards the end of the century, there is mention of a Russian merchant, Semen Malen'kij (Malinkov), being dispatched to Agra and Delhi by Peter the Great on an ostensible trade mission but again without success.[30] While Mughal power declined and was eventually replaced by the British *rāj*, the Russian state expanded into Central Asia and the two empires—the British and the Russian—entered into a period of conflict.

There was no real threat to the British, however, until, under Alexander III, Russian suzerainty was extended over the khanates of Central Asia bordering the Oxus region and Afghanistan.[31] Although we cannot review here the subsequent history of Russo-Indian diplomatic relations, mention should be made of Napoleon's plan for a joint Franco-Russian invasion of India. Tsar' Paul I decided, however, to act alone and in January of 1801 orders were issued for 22,000 Cossacks with artillery to march to Orenburg and thence to Bokhara and the Indus. But in March Paul was assassinated and the Cossacks were recalled.[32] A similar project was conceived of later during the Crimean War but, with the conclusion of hostilities, the plan was abandoned.[33]

4

In the eighteenth century we see continued consolidation of the extant information concerning India; there was, moreover, a significant expansion of this body of knowledge, and the groundwork was laid for the more exact and thorough studies of the following century. The major development in this connection was the work of William (later Sir William) Jones who first came to India in 1783 as a puisne judge of the Supreme Court at Fort William in Bengal. The Governor-General, Warren Hastings, wishing to rule his subjects in accordance with Indian law, commissioned a number of pandits to make a compilation of the Sanskrit legal texts. These were first rendered into Persian and then published in English as *The Code of Gentoo Law* (London, 1776).[34] Jones, who already knew a number of oriental languages, began the study of Sanskrit and, in 1784, was instrumental in founding the Asiatic Society of Bengal. In 1789 he translated Kālidāsa's classical drama, *Śakuntalā*, and in 1792 his edition of the *Ṛtusaṃhāra* ("Cycle of the Seasons") was published in Calcutta—the first printing of a Sanskrit text. In 1794 Jones completed his translation of *The Lawbook of Manu*. Prior to this, Charles Wilkins of the East India Company translated the *Bhagavadgītā* into English (the first translation of a Sanskrit work into English) and this was published in London in 1785.[35]

Jones is the recognized founder of Indology and was the first to state definitively the relationship between Sanskrit, Greek, and Latin as well as the probable affinity of Sanskrit with such languages as Persian, German, and Celtic. Even before coming to India he had recognized the connection between Persian and the European languages and he had rejected the fatuous notion that all these languages derived from Hebrew. But, as noted in the previous section, Stevens had earlier recognized certain linguistic affinities and the same discovery was made by the Italian merchant Sasseti in Goa.

Indeed, comparative Indo-European philology had been pioneered as early as the twelfth century by Geraldus Cambrensis who noticed similarities between Welsh, Greek, and Latin. J.J. Scaliger in his *Diatribe on the Languages of the Europeans* (1610) divided the IE languages into *matrices*, depending on the different words for "god". Marcus Boxhorn, a Dutch scholar, developed a "Scythian" theory of the common origin of the IE languages, a notion later taken up by Leibniz who also attacked the Hebraic hypothesis. At the beginning of the eighteenth century J. Lidoff, after a study of the Semitic languages, recognized the particular importance of inflectional forms in comparative philological studies. The Saxon missionary Ziegenbalg compiled his *Grammatica Damulica* in 1716 and the German Jesuit, Johannes Hanxleden, who lived in India from 1699 to 1732, was (it appears) the first European to compile a Sanskrit grammar. Although this was not published, it was utilized by an Austrian missionary who had his two Sanskrit grammars printed at Rome in 1790. In 1740 the Italian Jesuit, Constantino Beschi, came to Madura in southern India. He dressed in native costume, took a Tamil name, and learned Tamil so well that eventually he wrote an epic poem in the language—the "Thembavani".

So far as literary texts are concerned, the French scholar Anquetil-Duperron (who did not know Sanskrit) discovered the *Avesta* and published the *Zend-Avesta* in 1771. Later he acquired a Persian translation of the Upaniṣads; these he translated into a strange mixture of Latin, Greek, and Persian in 1796 and this work, which he entitled *Oupnekhat*, was printed in Paris, 1801-1802. The *Ezour Vedam* (i.e., the *Yajur Veda*), which appeared in 1778 and which caught the attention of Voltaire, turned out to be a 17th-18th-century Christian compilation. Jones' "Shakuntala" went into five editions in less than twenty years and Goethe became acquainted with this Sanskrit classic through Georg Forster's German version (from the English) of 1791.[36] His enthusiasm was expressed in the well-known epigram on the drama ("Sakontala"):

Willst Du die Blüte des frühen, die Früchte des
/späteren Jahres,
Willst Du was reizt und entzückt, willst du was
/sättigt und nährt,
Willst Du den Himmel, die Erde, mit Einem Namen
/begreifen;
Nenn'ich Sakontala, Dich, und so ist Alles gesagt.[37]

Furthermore, Goethe adapted a convention of Indian drama in the *Śakuntalā* for the Prologue to *Faust* and it is possible that the final chorus of the second part was inspired by Indian monism.

In 1814 Horace Wilson (who later became Boden Professor of Sanskrit at Oxford) translated Kālidāsa's poem, *Meghadūta* ("The Cloud Messenger"), which also came to the attention of Goethe.[38] But still greater interest in Sanskrit language and literature was stimulated at the beginning of the nineteenth century by Alexander Hamilton of the East India Company. While traveling through France on his return from India, he was detained in Paris in 1802 after the outbreak of the Napoleonic wars. Hamilton occupied his time examining and cataloguing the Indian manuscripts in the Bibliothèque Nationale and teaching Sanskrit. Among his students was Friedrich von Schlegel who learned to read Sanskrit and became intensely enamored of Indic culture: "Hier" (he wrote to Tieck in 1803) "ist eigentlich die Quelle aller Sprachen, aller Gedanken und Gedichte des menschlichen Geistes; *alles, alles stammt aus Indien* ohne Ausnahme".[39] Some years later in Germany Schlegel published his famous *Ueber die Sprache und Weisheit der Indier* (1808), while his brother, August, who had also learned Sanskrit, eventually became the first professor of Sanskrit in the West (Bonn, 1818). A contemporary of his, Franz Bopp, also studied Sanskrit in Paris and London and, with the publication of his *Ueber das Conjugationssystem der Sanskritsprache in Vergleichung mit jenem der griechischen, lateinischen, persischen und germanischen Sprache* in 1816, became the founder of comparative philology. Thereafter and down to the present day the names of German Sanskrit scholars are legion and "Sanskrit research has since been pursued in Germany with more zeal and success than in any other European country" (A.A. Macdonell).

The work of Jones, who died in 1794, was carried on by H.T. Colebrooke, a lawyer and a member of the East India Company. He came to India in 1782, took up the study of Sanskrit, and devoted himself to the study of Sanskrit literature. He wrote a surprisingly large number of essays and studies on Indian law, philosophy, religion, astronomy, mathematics, and grammar and was the first scholar to give a rather accurate account of the Vedas in 1805. He edited Pāṇini's famous Sanskrit grammar and wrote a grammar of his own. Colebrooke was followed by a continuous line of eminent British Sanskritists. Mention might also be made here of the publication in London in 1789 of what is very probably the first European novel set in India: this was *Hartly House Calcutta* by an anonymous English author, presumably a lady.[40]

There were also, following Anquetil-Duperron, some important French names in Sanskrit studies. Antoine Léonard de Chézy, at first a student of Persian, so admired Sir William Jones' translation of the *Śakuntalā* that he began the study of Sanskrit in order to be able to read the original. This he was soon able to do and he eventually published his own text of Kālidāsa's play. In 1814 he was the first orientalist to hold the chair of Sanskrit at the College de France. De Chézy was succeeded in 1832 by an even greater scholar, Eugène Burnouf, a recognized authority on Indian Buddhism. There then followed such eminent men as Foucaux, Hippolyte Fauche, Sylvain Lévi, Alfred Foucher, Jean Przyluski, Jules Bloch, Louis Renou, and Jean Filliozat—to name only a few.

5

Russian Indology begins with the arrival in India in 1785 of a Russian musician and adventurer, Gerasim Stepanovich Lebedev.[41] Lebedev (of whom little was known until fairly recently) learned some Sanskrit and Bengali and, in 1795, staged in Calcutta a comedy, adapted from Richard Jodrell's *The Disguise*, which he had himself translated into Bengali. He is thus considered the founder of modern Bengali theater.[42] This Bengali play was thought to have been lost until 1956 when a collection of documents relating to Lebedev's Indian career was published in the Soviet Academy of Sciences' *Istoricheskij arkhiv*; this contains a selection of Lebedev's papers (with an Introduction by K.A. Antonova) and Lebedev's Bengali translation of *The Disguise*.[43] But Lebedev, who knew English, had a *Grammar of the Pure and Mixed East Indian Dialects* published in London in 1801; he is also the author of *Bespristrastnoe sozertsanie sistem Vostochnoj Indii bramgenov, svjashchennykh obrjadov ikh i narodnykh obychaev* (St. Petersburg, 1805). He also cast, by order of Alexander I, the first Devanāgarī type in Russia. Not much is known about Lebedev's activities after his return to Russia in 1797; he is buried in the *Georgievskoe kladbishche* in Moscow.

Prior to Lebedev's arrival in India, however, the German orientalist T.S. Bayer, who came to Russia in 1726, had taken up the study of Sanskrit with the help of an Indian resident in St. Petersburg and published his *Elementa litteraturae Brachmanicae* in 1728.[44] Ten years later he published a history of the Greeks in Bactria entitled *Historia regni graecorum Bactriani*. Robert Lents (Lenz), who studied Sanskrit with Franz Bopp, published a number of Sanskrit studies, including *Analyse du Lalitavistara-pourana* (St. Petersburg, 1836).[45] A Russian version of Wilkins' *Bhagavadgītā* was published by N.I. Novikov in 1788 and in 1811 a short survey of the affinities between Sanskrit and Russian appeared in St. Petersburg in both French and Russian ("Rapports entre la langue sanskrite et la langue russe"). Lents, the first scholar to lecture on Sanskrit and Sanskrit literature in St. Petersburg, was succeeded by Pavel Petrov (d. 1875) who taught Sanskrit at the University of Kazan' and, later, at Moscow. Petrov was especially interested in the history of Kashmir and he translated the first book of Kalhaṇa's *Rājataraṅgiṇī*, published in 1865. Ivan Pavlovich Minaev (d. 1890), a student of the Sinologist V.P. Vasil'ev, became especially interested in Buddhism and studied Sanskrit at the University of St. Petersburg and in Germany under Weber and Benfey. In 1869 he was appointed Reader in Sanskrit Literature and in later years was a professor in the Department of Comparative Grammar of the Indo-European Languages at St. Petersburg University. In addition to his visits to Western Europe, Minaev made three trips to India; an account of the first of these was published in 1878 as *Ocherki Tsejlona i Indii, iz putevykh zametok russkogo*. Academician Barannikov discusses Minaev's scholarly accomplishments and enumerates his publications.[46] One of these, a study of A. Nikitin's *Khozhenie* (see above, section 3), will be referred to in the following chapter.

During the period 1852-1875 the monumental seven-volume St. Petersburg Sanskrit-German Dictionary (the "St. Petersburg Lexicon") was produced under the direction of the German scholar Rudolf Roth and the Russian scholar Otto Nikolaevich Betlingk and published by the Russian Imperial Academy of Sciences. A student of Minaev's, S.F. Ol'denburg, founded the *Bibliotheca Buddhica* in 1897, and another student, F.I. Shcherbatskoj (d. 1941), edited numerous Sanskrit and Tibetan texts for the *Bibliotheca*.[47] The continued interest of Russian—including Soviet—scholars in Indian and Sanskrit studies is apparent when one glances through professional journals and commemorative volumes.[48] Thus in a recent *Festschrift* in honor of the Dutch scholar, F.B.J. Kuiper, there are contributions by several Soviet Sanskritists.[49] Soviet scholars have also been active in studies of and attempts to decipher the Indus Valley Proto-Indian script and texts; there recently appeared an analysis and evaluation of their work by American specialists.[50]

More will be said about recent Soviet Sanskrit and Indian studies as well as other present-day relations between India and the Soviet Union at the end of Chapter V in this book. In marked contrast, however, to the generally high level of Soviet Indological research, especially in the area of Sanskrit, stands Soviet journalism which takes every opportunity, as one might expect, both to decry the vices of British and American imperialism and to vaunt the friendship that is supposed to exist between the Indian and Russian peoples. Newspaper articles along this line were particularly frequent just before and after the visit of the Prime Minister, Indirā Gāndhī, to Moscow in 1976. Reviews in Soviet periodicals dealing with books on India almost always castigate foreign imperialism, the brunt of the obloquy being directed again at the British and Americans. Thus in a recent review in *Novyj Mir* (No. 1, 1978) of a book by the Soviet journalist O. Orestov ("The Gates of India") the reviewer tells of the author's first visit to Calcutta in 1944 and his displeasure at the contrast between the starving populace on the one hand and the "lanky American soldiers, bursting with health" and the "spit-and-polish British officers" on the other. Ocasionally, too, articles by leftist Indian journalists outdo the Russians in sheer malice. For example, in the November, 1974, issue of the Indian magazine, *Bhavan's Alpha Monthly*, there appeared an unsigned article entitled "Gulag Again" in which it is suggested that *Gulag Archipelago* was not written by Solzhenitsyn but is actually a patch-work of notes left by Dr. Goebbels. Reading such hack journalism, one is reminded, however, of somewhat similar invective in the British press of the early nineteenth century concerning Imperial Russia. In, for instance, the 1838 volume of *Parbury's Oriental Herald*, a kind of gazette for the British in India, we read :

> The question of Russian power is momentous to the entire world. It is at once, and in the fewest words, Despotism arrayed against Freedom—Barbarism against Civilisation...Treaties to her are so many means of deception. She uses them to mask over her designs. The political, or more correctly, the moral principle of other nations she distorts to her advantage...The very essence of Russian polity, the last analysis it is possible to reduce it to, is despotism the most hideous imagination to its limits can conceive.

CHAPTER II

EARLY RUSSIAN LITERATURE

1

In this chapter we shall mention and discuss briefly those works of Old Russian literature and of the seventeenth century which contain references to India, which have their ultimate origin in India, or which relate in any way to Indian thought. We shall begin with the Alexander Romance.[1] It is impossible to determine precisely when and where the earliest Church Slavonic versions of the Alexander Romance (*Aleksandrija*, *Povest' ob Aleksandre Makedonskom*) first appeared. There are, however, reasons to believe that the earliest translations date from the eleventh century, although the extant texts date from the fifteenth and later centuries.[2] In the thirteenth century some unknown compiler in northeastern Russia produced the so-called "Second Redaction" of the *Aleksandrija*, introducing certain fantastic elements (concerning, e.g., India) from such works as the *Skazanie ob indijskom tsarstve* and the *Khozhenie Zosimy k rakhmanam* (see below) and giving new emphasis to such matters as the implacability of fate and the transitoriness of earthly success. Thus, as the Western versions of the Romance picture Alexander as the "perfect knight" in both his upbringing and his behavior, so the Slavic adaptations give the legend a marked ethical and religious coloration. These revisions and additions especially concern the portrayal of the characters of Alexander himself and of Darius; they are clearly seen in the conversations between the former and the *rakhmane* (i.e., the Brāhmaṇas, who are also referred to as the *nagomudretsy*, i.e., *gymnosophistai*[3]), particularly *Dan'damij*.[4] This revised *Aleksandrija* was included in the thirteenth-century "Hellenic Chronograph" (*Ellinskij letopisets*). D. Chizhevskij refers to this version of the *Aleksandrija* as an early forerunner of such later works as the novels of Dostoevskij and Tolstoj (especially *Resurrection*[5]). Beginning in the fifteenth century further revisions of the Alexander legend were made on the basis of new translations of Greek versions done in Serbia which occasionally reflect the influence of the Western Alexander Romance.[6] This highly romanticized *serbskaja Aleksandrija* introduces quite sentimental elements in, for instance, the passages describing Alexander's relations with his Persian wife, Roxana. Although there is no hard evidence, it is possible that certain tropes (actually calques from the Greek) in the early *Aleksandrija* had some influence on the language of the *Slovo o polku Igoreve* (c. 1187).[7]

The *Skazanie ob indijskom tsarstve* (*Skazanie ob Indii bogatoj*)—which is also frequently mentioned in connection with the *Slovo*[8]—was in effect originally the Slavonic version of the story of Prester John and his feudal utopia—more accurately, the apocryphal "Letter of Prester John". The Slavonic text appeared in the late twelfth or early thirteenth century, a translation in this case from a Latin version produced earlier in Dalmatia. The Byzantine "Story of the Indian Kingdom" served, it appears, as a political pamphlet; the Slavonic version, too, while reflecting the marked interest in fabulous accounts of the East, seems to have had political overtones (allusions perhaps to certain tensions between church and state). Like the earlier and Western versions, the *Skazanie* is replete with accounts of strange men and animals, precious gems, incredible geographical features, and, of course, of the vastness and power of King John's Indian domains. In this connection, the hyperbolic descriptions of India and its inhabitants clearly establish an "India the Rich" topos. Afanasij Nikitin (see below) may have made use of the descriptions in the *Skazanie* in his *Khozhenie*. The original form of the *Skazanie* has not come down to us; what we have are those segments included in the second redaction of the *Aleksandrija*, as mentioned above. Although our texts of the *starina* concerning Djuk Stepanovich, beginning (in one version),

> Vo toj bylo Indii vo bogatyja
> A byl molodoj bojarin Djuk Stepanovich,[9]

are of much later date, the narrative is apparently very old and shows some features similar to the *Skazanie ob Indii bogatoj*.[10]

The "Tale of the Dreams of King Shakhajsha" (*Povest' o snakh tsarja Shakhajshi* or *Skazanie o dvenadtsati snakh tsarja Shakhajshi*) also appears to be of ultimately Indian origin, although, as mentioned in the preceding chapter, there is no extant Byzantine Greek version. It is very likely, however, that the Slavic version first appeared in Dalmatia and was a translation from a lost Greek original.[11] The Indian—and especially Buddhist—provenance of the Tale is to some extent corroborated by the existence of a Tibetan account of a king and twelve dreams as well as similar incidents in Arabic and Syrian sources. The many extant copies of this *Povest'* date from the fifteenth century and later and are in two variants, one of which puts the name of the sage and dream-interpreter Mamer in the title in place of Shakhajsha. The generally dark tone of the Tale, the ominous dreams of the coming of "evil times", and the eschatological allusions all indicate what must have been widespread and similar feelings amongst the Russian populace during and after the *tatarshchina*.

2

In the preceding chapter we discussed briefly the background of the Greek work known as *Barlaam kai Ioasaph* (Barlaam and Ioasaph, or Josaphat): its possible authorship, the Indian—more specifically, Pali—origins of at least portions of the narrative, the Christianization of the romance, and its wide dissemination and influence in later literatures of the West. Those portions of the Greek text of oriental provenance derive, possibly via a Georgian version,[12] from an Arabic text and this in turn derives from a Persian translation of a Pali original done in the sixth or seventh century.[13] The Slavonic version was produced in Kiev in the eleventh century, although there might have been earlier Bulgarian translations of particular episodes. The Greek text, which was incorporated by Simeon Metaphrastes in his *Lives of the Saints* (10th century), was translated into Latin prior to the twelfth century and thence into the other languages of Europe.

Although the oldest Russian copy of the *Povest' o Varlaame i Ioasafe* dates from the fourteenth or fifteenth century,[14] some of the apologues (*pritchi*) seem to have been known even before the complete translation appeared; these were included in the twelfth-century *Prolog* (i.e., synaxarion or menologion), or collection of short lives of the saints with the addition of various *pritchi*. One of Kirill of Turov's symbolic tales (12th century) takes its plot from a *Barlaam and Josaphat* apologue: a *tsar'* is forced to flee his realm and seeks safety in a cave filled with arms and where a man is carousing with a woman over a bottle of wine. Kirill interprets the tale at length: the realm or kingdom is man's body, the *tsar'* is man's soul, the cave is a monastery, the arms are spiritual arms, etc.[15] Kirill also has another tale of Indian origin that is familiar in the West as the "Parable of the Blind and the Lame". A landlord (i.e., God) places two men, one lame (the Soul) and one blind (the Body), in charge of his vineyard. Individually they cannot both steal and flee, but when the lame man sits on the back of the blind man and shows him the way, they are successful. Thus sin is possible through the cooperation, so to speak, of body and soul. In the fifteenth century some versions of the *Povest'* underwent the "Athanasian recension" (*Afanas'evskij izvod*),[16] i.e., they reflect the tendency to give primacy to the spiritual or theocratic power of the state and to minimize secular power, a tendency particularly associated with Joseph (Sanin) of Volokolamsk and the "Josephites" (opposed by the "Trans-Volgans").[17]

By the seventeenth century the *Povest'* was being interpreted as actual hagiography.[18] It also reached the Ukraine (where the story has always been popular[19]) and Simeon Polotskij published in Moscow a new version, revised on the basis of the Latin text. Another of the apologues turns up occasionally in various forms in the modern literatures: this is the story of the traveler, pursued by a unicorn (*edinorog*; Skt *ekaśṛṅga*), who seeks safety in a ravine; but in the ravine there is a dragon and the traveler holds tightly to a shrub on the side of the ravine (in some versions he is also threatened by asps and by mice who loosen the roots of the shrub); but he discovers wild honey and when he tastes this he forgets his predicament. In Russian literature Lev Tolstoj uses this story in his *Ispoved'* (IV).[20]

In the Slavic versions of the Byzantine animal fable, *Stephanitēs kai Ichnilatēs*, we have a direct though remote connection with the *Pañcatantra*. As noted in the preceding chapter, Symeon Seth produced the Greek translation in the eleventh century; this Greek text was first translated in Bulgaria: one version reached the East Slavs in the twelfth or thirteenth century and another in the fourteenth or fifteenth. The oldest manuscript of *Stefanit i Ikhnilat* dates from 1478.[21] The story, which was very popular (A.M. Remizov calls it "ljubimaja kniga moskovskoj Rusi XVI i XVII vekov"), is simple: two jackals falsely accuse the bull before King Lion; first the bull dies and then the two jackals die.[22]

But the narrative is embellished with many moralizing fables, all involving various animals. The story is mentioned in the *Novaja povest'* of 1610, and in 1762 Boris Volkov made a new translation from the French: *Politicheskie i nravouchitel'nye basni Pil'paja, filosofa indijskogo.*[23] The Slavic texts of *Stefanit i Ikhnilat* were published by the "Obshchestvo ljubitelej drevnej pis'mennosti" in the late nineteenth century. In the twentieth century Aleksej Remizov wrote a stylized version of the story.[24]

The *Tolkovaja Paleja* (OT stories with commentaries) of 1477 as well as later *palei* contain the apocryphal *Povest' o Solomone i Kitovrase*; this tale had been translated from the Greek earlier in the Kievan period, although no such Byzantine work is now extant. As mentioned in the preceding chapter, the word *kitovras* may be derived from the Sanskrit *gandharva* and the tale itself—or some part of it—is generally considered to be of ultimately Indian origin.[25] Nor are there any South Slavic versions of the tale, although the Pogodin (Bulgarian) *Nomokanon* of the fourteenth century indicates their presence by warning: "o Solomone tsari i o Kitovrase basni i koshchuny—lgano; ne byval Kitovras na zemli, no èllinskie filosofy vveli".[26] The story tells of Solomon's need for the *kitovras* (in Talmudic legend, Asmadai) in order to find the *shamir* in order, in turn, to secure the stone for building the Temple.[27] Kitovras entered Russian folklore and legend as a creature that could move only in one direction (as described in the *Povest'*) and we find him in the *byliny* (e.g., on Vasilij Okulevich). The French scholar A. Vaillant recognizes Kitovras under a different name in a Serbian folktale,[28] while the Russian classicist and symbolist poet, Vjacheslav Ivanov (d. 1949), has a poem entitled *Kitovras*; but here Kitovras is a Pan-like creature much like the Kitovras in some verses by Sergej Gorodetskij used by Ivanov as an epigraph.[29]

Also included in the thirteenth-century "Hellenic Chronograph", mentioned above in connection with the *Aleksandrija*, were two other works relating to India. One of these is the *Khozhdenie Zosimy k rakhmanam* (*Khozhdenie v zemnoj raj pravednogo pustynnika Zosimy*).[30] Indeed, matter from this work was incorporated in the second redaction of *Aleksandrija* as well as in the fourteenth-century *Poslanie arkhiepiskopa Novgorod'skogo Vasilija ko vladytse Tferskomu Feodoru.*[31] The *Khozhdenie Zosimy*, which appears to have been translated from an unknown Greek or

Latin source, is classified as "utopian" by Chizhevskij, describing as it does the sinless, meatless, and quite idyllic life of the *rakhmane.*[32] Such descriptions go back very clearly to the ancient Greek accounts of the *Brachmanes* and *gymnosophistai.* The other work (its source is also unknown) included in the "Hellenic Chronograph" is the *Khozhdenie trekh inokov k Makariju.* This tale, which seems to be a compilation, presents grim pictures of hell with the addition of fantastic scenes involving those grotesque men and animals which had always, from the very first occidental contacts with India, been part of the accounts of writers and travelers.

We find further accounts of the *rakhmane* in the *Slovo o rakhmanakh i ikh predivnom zhitii* included in the fifteenth-century *paleja* of the monk Evfrosin (which also contains the *Povest' o Solomone i Kitovrase*); in this case the descriptions come from the *Chronika* of Georgios Monachos (Hamartolos).[33] There is actually only passing mention of the Rakhmans as philosophers in the Russian version of Cosmas Indicopleustes' *Christian Topography* (*Kniga glagolemaja Koz'my Indikoplova*)[34] and again the reference (in the original Greek) is based, as noted in the preceding chapter, on hearsay. The Greek text was first translated in Kievan Russia as early as the twelfth century, although no extant copies are earlier than the fifteenth century. The Russian manuscripts, like the Greek, contain numerous illustrations which make graphic the author's strange Ptolemaic and Biblical cosmology.[35] In the thirteenth century excerpts from the *Topography* were included in the *Iudejskij khronograf* reviewing Jewish history from Adam to the conquest of Jerusalem by Vespasian; and in the sixteenth century the Metropolitan Makarij also included passages in his new "Reading Menaea" (*Chet'i-minei*).[36]

It may be of interest to note here that the word *rakhman* entered the Russian onomasticon in the form *rakhmanin*; the late Boris Unbegaun writes:

> The surname Rakhmaninov perhaps belongs to the same type of name, deriving from OR *rachmanin* "Indian" *brahman*, through a Byzantine intermediary. The term is not uncommon in Old Russian literary works, for example, in the OR *Alexandriad.* There is, however, the OR adjective *rachmannyj* "tame, lazy, gay, jovial", which may or may not be of the same origin. A first name Rachman also occurs in Old Russian. Whatever

the origin of *rachmanin*, it was probably used as a nickname rather than as a national name.[37]

3

In 1466 a Russian merchant of Tver', Afanasij Nikitin, and a number of other merchants sailed from Nizhnij Novgorod to Astrakhan'. Here the group was attacked and robbed by Tatars but released with their two ships. During a storm on the Caspian one ship was wrecked and the other, carrying Nikitin, reached Derbent. Nikitin then went on to Baku, sailed to Chebokar (Chapokur), and moved south into Persia where he remained for two years. In 1469 he sailed from Moskat to Cambay in the Gulf of Cambay in Gujarat. He remained in India for three years (1469-1472).

Nikitin wrote an account, almost wholly devoted to India, of his travels, and his manuscript, which he never really put into finished form (he died on his return but before he reached Tver'), was later incorporated in a chronicle (*II Sofijskaja letopis'*, 1475). This work is known as the *Khozhenie za tri morja*, the "three seas" being the Caspian Sea, the Indian Ocean, and the Black Sea (which he crossed on his return journey).[38] A sixteenth-or seventeenth-century copy (the *Troitskij spisok*) was discovered by N.M. Karamzin early in the nineteenth century and later additional copies were found.

From a sophisticated literary point of view, the *Khozhenie* is, frankly speaking, rather crude. Soviet scholars, of course, laud its simplicity and "proletarian" features, while others express less enthusiasm for it as a literary work. Thus Chizhevskij writes that "its significance for literature is strongly over-emphasized by modern scholars".[39] In any case, however, since it is traditional to speak of the "literature of travel" (even when such works are pedestrian and boring), the *Khozhenie* cannot be ignored; nor, because of its very apparent historical, ethnological, and linguistic significance, should it be.[40]

Nikitin traveled in predominantly Muslim India and he does not mention the Rakhmans. But he describes carved figures of Hindu gods—e.g., Gaṇeśa (*drugoe chelovek, a nos slonov*) and Hanumān (*tret'e chelovek, a viden'e obez'anino*). And he mentions "statues of the Buddha" (*Buty*) and Buddhist temples which he calls (using a Persian word) *butkhany* or "houses of idols", the remains of the much earlier Buddhist period in India.[41] A number of Muslim rites and festivals are also described and Nikitin quite frequently uses Arabic, Persian, and Turkish words and phrases which reflect his own smattering of linguistic knowledge in these areas. Petrushevskij refers to these passages as representing a kind of "Volapük" or "macaronic language", a quaint mixture of Arabic, Persian, and Turkish lexical elements.[42] For the most part, Nikitin's descriptions appear to be based on his own observations, but occasionally he will tell us about such things as the *gukuk* bird (when it alights on a house, someone there will die, and if one tries to kill it, fire will issue from its beak) or the "Kingdom of the Apes", the *knjaz' obez'jan'skyj*, the ape army, and an ape language.[43] Such stories may be based on hearsay or they may have been inserted by Nikitin from his own store of misinformation concerning "India the fabulous" culled from such earlier works as the *Skazanie ob indijskom tsarstve*.

4

In the sixteenth century another collection of tales, the *Istorija semi mudretsov*, appeared, having been translated, probably from Polish, in Belorussia. The Polish version stems in turn from a Latin translation (*Historia septem sapientium Romae*) of the thirteenth century which was itself translated from a Hebrew text. From there the narrative goes back via Greek, Syriac, Arabic, and Persian versions to an Indian original source which has never been found.[44] The oldest Russian MS of the *Istorija*, dated 1634, was destroyed in the Moscow fire of 1812, but more than seventeen copies are extant. The *Istorija* begins with a tale about a prince (*Diokletian*) who is to be executed by his father (King Eliazar) on the basis of an accusation brought by the stepmother. Each of the seven sages (under whom the prince has been studying) tells the king an apologue or moral tale in order to save the prince; and the stepmother answers each of these with a narrative of her own.[45] The *Istorija* contains fifteen of these "novellas". One tale has become quite familiar, especially in the West (with minor variations): this is the one recounted by the first sage. There was, the story runs, a brave knight with a much-beloved son attended by three nurses. The knight also had a favorite dog and a falcon. The knight and his wife are invited to a feast and they leave the child in the care of one nurse who then retires, leaving the dog and the falcon to guard the cradle. A snake approaches the cradle and is about to bite the child, when the falcon awakens the dog and the latter kills the serpent. But the cradle is broken and collapses in the struggle and much blood is spilt. When the knight returns, he assumes of course that the dog has attacked and devoured the child, and in anger he kills the dog who had run to meet him. Then the concealed but unharmed infant is found and the knight regrets his hasty conclusion.[46]

The *Skazanie* (or *Povest'*) *o Eruslane Lazareviche* (or *Uruslane Zalazoreviche*) is of Persian rather than Indian provenance. It makes its first appearance early in the seventeenth century, having reached the Slavs (probably the Cossacks) via Turkish versions of two episodes out of the Persian epic, the *Shahnameh* of Firdousi.[47] The hero of the *skazanie*, Uruslan (<Turk. Arslan), the Rustem of the Persian poem, does, however, visit the Indian Kingdom. Here Uruslan slays a three-headed monster inhabiting a lake and due soon to devour the Indian king's daughter. As a reward, the king gives his daughter in marriage to Uruslan. But the latter learns of a "most beautiful queen" in the "City of the Sun"[48] and he abandons his wife on their wedding night to search for her. He tells the Indian princess that, should she bear a son, she must give him a certain jewel. Uruslan finds the queen and lives with her until his son by the Indian princess, Uruslan Uruslanovich, comes searching for his father. The father recognizes his son by the jewel and they return to the Indian Kingdom where Uruslan is given half the realm to rule. The younger Uruslan goes off as a *bogatyr'*. With variations, this tale becomes a popular fable and the subject of *lubki* during the eighteenth century.[49] Pushkin later used a purely Russian version of the Uruslan/Ruslan tale in his *Ruslan i Ljudmila*.

The archpriest Avvakum (the name derives, via the Greek, from the Hebrew Habhaqquk), who was born about 1620 and who was burned at the stake as an heretical Old Believer in 1682, is an important figure in seventeenth-century Russian letters. Though neither his writings nor his theology is ever related to Hindu or Buddhist thought, there is one aspect of his work that is intriguing—this is the occasional reference (e.g., in his *Beseda o staroljubtsakh i novoljubtsakh*) to self-immolation (*samosozhzhenie*). Articles on this topic, such as that by G. Hildebrandt,[50] do not mention any possible Indian influence; yet one cannot help recalling in this connection the ancient accounts (e.g., that of Bardesanes) of the holy men who practiced self-immolation, as well as the Buddhists of Southeast Asia who still occasionally do the same.

The name of Simeon Polotskij was mentioned earlier as having published a new version, revised on the basis of Latin texts, of the *Povest' o Varlaame i Ioasafe.* This appeared in Moscow in 1681, a year after Polotskij's death.[51] Polotskij, a Ukrainian by birth, is a major figure of the Russian baroque with a stronger background in Latin literature and the Latin Church Fathers than in Slavonic literature. His baroque style is amply illustrated in, for example, his *Orel rossijskij,* a panegyric written in 1667 on the occasion of the thirteenth birthday of the tsarevich (Aleksej Mikhajlovich). Like Milton, the Russian poets of the seventeenth and eighteenth centuries mixed classical and oriental imagery, while the riches of India had long since become proverbial. Thus Polotskij, amongst the many other hyperboles in this poem, boldly links the Ganges (*Gaṅgā*) with the Pactolus as a gold-bearing river; but neither river, the poet asserts, bears so much gold as the tsarevich shows traits of kindness.[52] But the minor poets of the seventeenth century also like to allude to the riches—especially the jewels—of India and a good example is afforded by such a reference in Andrej Belobotskij's *Pentateugum.* We might also mention here that in the *Artakserksovo dejstvo* or "Comedy of Artaxerxes" (1672) by Pastor Gregory, although the plot involves the Biblical story of Esther and Ahasuerus, India is referred to by Haman:

> Persida i Indeja
> i inye gosudarstva ne smejut mi protivitis'.[53]

Less frequently India and its "devilish practices" are related to evil. In the anonymous seventeenth-century demonological tale, *Povest' o Savve Grudtsyne* (which is extant in numerous versions), Savva visits the palace and throne-room of the Prince of Darkness where he sees several winged youths with blue, red, and black faces. The demon who accompanies Savva explains that many nations serve Satan—*indei, persy i inii mnozi.* (These details are retained in the modern retelling of the tale by Aleksej Remizov who adds, however, the Chinese and the Ethiopians.[54]) Antony

Stokes, commenting on this passage in the story, writes: "The strange blend of medieval credulity and naive attempts at realism are very characteristic of this transitional period".[55] But we may have here echoes of travelers' accounts of the variously colored representations of the Hindu deities and demigods.

5

The question of Indian Buddhist influence on early Russian religious thought is a difficult one to answer in other than very general statements of possibility.[56] Though the ascetic practices of the Indian śramaṇas were noted and described in considerable detail by the Greeks; and though such phenomena continued to be mentioned in many subsequent accounts, both real and fictional, of India, narratives of ultimately Indian (Buddhist and Hindu) origin, whether or not they referred to ascetic practices, were in any case supplemented in Kievan Russia with ethical and eremitical details. As Father Mahoney writes:

> One must also remember that the only literature available to the Russians at the time was that of an ascetical nature. Practically all of the ancient literature found in Russia between the 11th to the 15th centuries is of a translated nature from southern Slavic countries through Slavonic translations. For those who knew how to read, selections from the Fathers, from the various *Pateriki*, Lives of the Saints and Sayings of the Martyrs were the sole source of literature. A simple example of the history of Varlaam and Ioasaf tsarevich, founded on the idealization of the hermit life, translated into Slavonic and brought into Russia, had such popularity that it came down in folk-poetry in verses about Asaf tsarevich and in general of praise for the monastic life. People read some each day, learned verses by heart, which entered into their views and convictions and were expressed in their practical activities by establishing and spreading of monastic hermitages in unpopulated areas of Russia.[57]

But the likelihood of Indian Buddhist influence on Byzantine and Russian hesychasm has been suggested. Thus G. Wunderle writes: "On peut vraisemblablement supposer qu'après le grand Siméon le Nouveau Théologien il y a eu dans sa technique psychologique des infiltrations d'élements empruntés à l'Extrême-Orient (ou mieux encore au Brahmanisme)".[58] On the whole, however, such matters as Buddhism, Hinduism, and Brāhmaṇism are more frequently mentioned in connection with later, nineteenth- and twentieth-century Russian writers and thinkers and more will be said of these matters in the following chapters.

But Russian hesychasm is sometimes associated with yoga. Several years ago a book by Dom Jean-Marie Déchanet appeared in English translation—*Christian Yoga.*[59] In an appendix Jean Gouillard, citing a reference by Father Déchanet to ancient Christian practices, mentions the *Philokalia* and the *startsy* (elders) of Eastern Orthodoxy. The *Philokalia* is a collection of texts (4th to 14th centuries) by Fathers of the Eastern Church largely concerned with contemplative prayer; it exists in several recensions, including a Russian version (*Dobrotoljubie*). It is interesting that Gouillard cites illustrative passages from a French translation of the Russian text, while the translator uses the English version of the same Russian text.[60] Appendix II of Dom Déchanet's book quotes extracts from the *Philokalia* reminiscent of yoga, such as this one from Mark the Anchorite:

> There can be no pacifying the intellect without also pacifying the body. The partition between them cannot be broken down without silence and prayer;

or this from St. John of the Ladder (Climacus):

> Silence of the body is obtained by understanding and control of external behaviour and the activity of the senses. Silence of the soul is achieved by knowing thoughts for what they are while remaining in inviolate possession of one's intellect.

Finally, in studies of Slavic mythology, pre-Christian Slavic religion, or the vestiges of paganism in Russian Orthodox Christianity, one occasionally encounters mention of India. Thus Marija Gimbutas in her paper, "Ancient Slavic Religion: A Synopsis",[61] refers to the early Slavs' likening time to a wheel-track and she compares the Common Slavic **verme* and the Old Indic *vartman.* V.N. Toporov in "Parallels to Ancient Indo-Iranian Social and Mythological Concepts"[62] finds reminiscences of Mithraic terminology in early Slavic and he traces certain parallels between the demon adversaries of Indra and the heroes of Russian folk-tales. In his *Religioznyj èkstaz v russkom misticheskom sektantstve* D.G. Konovalov notes some words (e.g., *purusha*, *diva*, *majja*) of apparently Sanskrit origin in the glossolalia of the Khlysty.[63]

CHAPTER III

THE EIGHTEENTH CENTURY

I

If we look for oriental themes and motifs in the literature—especially the prose—of eighteenth-century England, we shall find that, aside from occasional references to such things as Brāhmaṇas, the Ganges, and the Hindu gods, the great majority of topics refer to Persia and, even more frequently, to China. Eighteenth-century Europe:

> ...with its faith in Reason and its distrust of disorder, looked at China with admiration. It was natural that China should be so admired, as according to the Jesuit reports she had an orderly government with scholar-governors—the Mandarins—and above all Confucian political philosophy. The *philosophes* found in China a great civilization which owed nothing to the Greco-Roman heritage or to the Christian tradition...Voltaire admired China, particularly her political organization and her ethics based on Reason. His *Orphelin de la Chine* was largely written to prove Rousseau wrong. Rousseau thought that science and art are destructive of morals. Voltaire in his *Orphelin de la Chine* made an attempt to show that this was not so in China. In fact there was in Europe, in the eighteenth century, a cult of China; and Asia, as seen by the Rationalist thinkers, meant, primarily, China.
>
> India, by contrast, appeared disorderly, chaotic and superstitious. Her heterogeneous culture, her diverse customs and her loosely knitted empire were to the *philosophes* difficult to put into a rational order. The cunning and ritual-ridden Brahmins were no match for the Mandarins.[1]

A study of the oriental tale in England in the eighteenth century will corroborate this: one of the very few titles which refer to India is that of an unpublished MS of Laurence Sterne's—*The*

Bramine's Journal.[2] It must be remembered, however, that William Jones did not arrive in India until 1783 and that England and English writers paid little attention to the Orient in general or to India in particular until the era of colonial expansion had begun under the elder Pitt. Thereafter, and especially after Queen Victoria was declared Empress of India in 1877, India not only became the setting for works of English prose but also provided extensive imagery for English verse. In the case of German literature, A.L. Willson points out that the marked increase in accounts of travel in India during the second half of the eighteenth century provided the source of the "Romantic mythical image" of India in German romanticism.[3] As regards French literature, Pierre Martino, speaking mainly of other than Indian oriental influences, writes:

> La littérature chercha d'abord dans l'Orient, tel qu'elle le concevait, ce qui pouvait satisfaire l'imagination, et c'est par le théâtre, par le roman aussi que l'exotisme commença. La tragédie fut de tous les genres littéraires celui qui profita le premier des perspectives nouvelles ouvertes sur l'Asie. La comédie vint plus tard: pour se moquer de quelqu'un, il faut déja le connaitre assez bien. Le roman, à toute époque, au XVIIe et au XVIIIe siecle surtout, s'est développé en même temps que la tragédie et la comédie: il a reçu d'elles sa matière presque toujours, et souvent son esprit: l'Orient ne manqua xonc pas d'y faire figure, et avec les premières années du XVIIIe siècle, il s'y installa pour ne jamais l'abandonner.[4]

So far as Russia is concerned, the Caucasus and Central Asia eventually assumed a position relative to Russian literature comparable to that of India with respect to English literature. In eighteenth-century Russian literature, too, themes and motifs drawn from the Near and Far East outnumber those relating to India. I might cite, as examples of the *vostochnaja povest'*, such works as Krylov's philosophical tale, *Kaib* (1792) and Pavel L'vov's allegorical fantasy, *Khram istiny. Videnie Sezostrisa, tsarja egipetskogo* (1796)[5]. Fonvizin's *Kallisfen* (1786), although subtitled *grecheskaja povest'* by the author, involves Alexander's Persian expedition and is mentioned by Städtke as an "orientalische Erzählung".[6] Another work by Fonvizin indicates the period's marked interest in China—or rather *kitajshchina* (*chinoiserie*): this is the translation, published anonymously in 1779, of a French version of the Chinese classic, the *Ta Hsüeh* ("Great Learning" or "The Higher Education")—*Ta-Gio, ili Velikaja nauka, zakljuchajushchaja v sebe vysokuju kitajskuju filosofiju.*[7] There were also translations of many of Voltaire's *contes philosophiques*, including several relating to India, published in the journals—e.g., *Dobryj Bramin* (*Histoire d'un Bon Bramin*) in the *Sankt-Peterburgskij Vestnik* (V, No. 4, 1780).[8] It is interesting, by the way, that at the very beginning of the century one of the earliest editions of *Vedomosti*—indeed, the earliest copy that is extant (2 January, 1703)—carries an item on India: *Iz Persidy pishut, Indejskij tsar' poslal v darakh velikomu gosudarju nashemu slona i inykh veshchej nemalo. Iz grada Shemakhi otpushchen on v Astrakhan' sukhim putem.*[9] The elephant and the other gifts were presented to Peter the Great's mission, referred to above in Chapter I, by the Mughal King, Aurangzeb, but they never reached their destination.[10]

During the eighteenth century a number of works of Sanskrit literature were translated into Russian, usually via earlier French, German, or English versions. For example, in 1762 Boris Volkov's Russian version of the Fables of Pilpay, translated from the French, was published in St. Petersburg (*Politicheskie i nravouchitel'nye basni Pil'paja, filosofa indijskogo*); and in 1788 A. Petrov's translation from the English text of the *Bhagavadgītā* was published in Moscow (*Baguat-Geta ili besedy Krishny s Arjunom*). In 1792 N.M. Karamzin published in the *Moskovskij zhurnal* some scenes from Kālidāsa's *Śakuntalā*. Karamzin's Russian translation was based on Georg Forster's German version (1791) which was itself, as noted in Chapter I, based on Sir William Jones' English translation (1789). In a preface Karamzin wrote:

> On almost every page of this drama I found the most sublime poetic beauty, the most subtle feelings, a gentle, exquisite and ineffable tenderness, similar to a quiet May evening, to the purest, inimitable Nature, as well as very great art. Moreover, this may be called a most beautiful picture of ancient India, just as Homer's poems are a picture of ancient Greece.[11]

Other works related to India also appeared, such as the scholarly writings of T.S. Bayer, mentioned earlier in Chapter I, section

5. Particularly numerous in the second half of the century were articles and books on the geography and peoples of India (e.g., "Razhaputy" in *Rastushchij vinograd* January, 1786); on Russia's commercial relations with India (e.g., "Iz" jasnenie o sposobakh k proizvedeniju Rossijskoj kommertsii iz Orenburga s Bukharskoju, a iz onoj i s Indijskimi oblastjami" in *Ezhemesjachnye sochinenija i izvestija o uchenykh delakh*, St. P., November, 1763); and on British rule in India ("Opisanie zhizni bengal'skogo general-gubernatora Gastingsa" in Supplement to *Moskovskie vedomosti*, No. 13, 1784). Popular, too, were accounts—very often translations—of voyages to or travels in India. Serialized, for example, in *Detskoe chtenie dlja serdtsa i razuma* (numbers 35-39, Moscow, 1786) was a narrative of Vasco da Gama's voyage—"Puteshestvie Vasko da Gamy v Ost-Indiju". And in St. Petersburg there appeared in the same year (there were later two further editions) F.S. Efremov's *Rossijskogo unter-ofitsera, nyne kollezhskogo asessora, devjatiletnee stranstvovanie i prikljuchenija v Bukharii, Khive, Persii i Indii.*[12]

2

References to India are occasionally encountered in the oriental tales and novels of the eighteenth century. These may simply amount to the mention of a place-name or two, introduced to add an extra touch of exoticism. Thus in Sergej Glinka's oriental adventure romance, *Selim i Roksana* (1798), Roxana is the daughter of the "King of Kashmir".[13] In Fedor Émin's very popular novel, *Nepostojannaja Fortuna, ili pokhuzhdenija Miramonda* (1763), Miramond meets a young anchorite who turns out to be a "Kombajskij prints". This "Prince of Cambay" falls in love with Agata but, before approval of the marriage arrives from India, he contracts small-pox which disfigures his face and he gives up all hope of happiness. It is noteworthy, by the way, that M.D. Chulkov (1743-1792), the author of the well-known *Prigozhaja povarikha*, was also a civil servant who rose from a minor position in the *Kommerts-kollegija* to the rank of *nadvornyj sovetnik*. During the years 1781-1788 he produced the twenty-one volumes of his *Istoricheskoe opisanie rossijskoj kommertsii*. The second volume of this impressive series deals with India and was published in Moscow in 1785.[14]

In the poetry of the eighteenth century in Russia allusions to the wealth of India became commonplaces which persisted for decades. Thus Lomonosov, in an ode in honor of the accession of Elizaveta Petrovna to the throne in 1747, emphasizes Russia's wealth:

When the All-Highest handed
To Thee such extent of lands
In happy sovereignty,
Then did He reveal such riches
As India is famous for.

In another ode to Peter III in 1762 Lomonosov includes India amongst those lands which will eventually become subject to Russia's laws:

There roars with frozen wings
Boreas, father of dense snows,
And opens a path amidst the ice
For Thy will's way to the East
That China, India and Japan
Might subject be to Thy laws.[15]

And in his play, *Tamira i Selim* (1750), Lomonosov has Selim tell of his visit to India and the *mudrye Braminy*.

Often allusions to India appear in translations or adaptations of Latin verse, as in this line by N.N. Popovskij (cf. Horace, Odes 1.22):

Or where flow the waters of the Hydaspes,

or in P. Kapnist's version (in *Bezopasnost'*),

Where the marvelous Hydaspes flows.[16]

Among allusions to particular regions of India it is perhaps Kashmir—or the "Vale of Kashmir" (*dolina Kashemira*)—that occurs most frequently in Russian poetry. Such a reference occurs, for example, in Derzhavin's "Ode to Felitsa" (Catherine II) of 1782:

But where shines Thy throne here below?
Where, branch of Heaven, doest Thou bloom?
In Baghdad, in Smyrna or in Kashmir?

Kashmir is often associated with roses (as in Venevitinov's *Tri rozy*, 1826) and pictured as a paradise on earth.[17] We also find periphrastic references to such particular products of India as tea; thus Kantemir in his Satire II has

> You stretch out now an hour or two at ease, awaiting
> The drink that India sends or is brought from China.

And, of course, diamonds and rubies from the realm of the Grand Mogul:

> Mogolets shlet almaz, rubin

(Zhukovskij, *Mogushchestvo, slava i blagodejstvie Rossii*, 1799). Incidentally, words such as *mogolets*, *Mogol*, *Velikij Mogol* occur frequently in the verse of the eighteenth and early nineteenth centuries, often standing simply for *indeets*, *indijskij*, *Indija*, etc., as in Polezhaev's *Akhaluk* (1833):

> ...the flash of diamonds
> On the Mogul's turban...

This is quite natural, since the Mughal Empire, which lasted from 1526 to 1761, was essentially the India which so many Russian merchants and travelers had known and the India which the Imperial government had so often dealt with.

Vasilij Majkov (1728-1778) has, among his *nravouchitel' nye basni*, one fable of Indian origin entitled *Dvoe prokhozhikh i klad*, written between 1763 and 1767. This is an abbreviated version of a fable from Pilpay entitled, in Boris Volkov's translation from the French, *O dvukh puteshestvennikakh i o l've, sdelannom iz belogo kamnja*, which appeared in 1762. Two travelers reach a fairly narrow but swift and possibly deep stream. On the other side they see a statue with an inscription promising treasure to the one who dares to swim across the stream. One traveler considers the risks and does not venture to cross; the other dives in, swims to the other side, and gains the gold. The former traveler then comments:

> I see that Fortune does not consider us apart:
> Alike to sage and fool it gives reward.

Aleksandr Radishchev (1749-1802) mentions the gymnosophists and Brāhmaṇas in his essay, "O cheloveke, o ego smertnosti i bessmertii"; and, in his *Pesn' istoricheskaja* (1796), he refers to the Sanskrit language and to the *Yajurveda.* In the "Chudovo" section of his *Puteshestvie iz Peterburga v Moskvu* (1790) Radishchev concludes an account of the refusal of tsarist officials to assist some shipwrecked men with the words, *Ja vospomjanul o zakljuchennykh aglichanakh v temnitse bengal'skogo subaba.* The reference is, of course, as the author makes clear in a long note, to the notorious "Black Hole of Calcutta" incident which occurred in 1756 when the Mughal viceroy of Bengal, the Nawab (or Subab) Suraj-ud-Dowla, captured Calcutta and put 146 British soldiers into a very small cell; only twenty-three men survived.[18]

Published in St. Petersburg in 1766 was a Russian translation (from a German version) of a work by the prominent Danish writer, Ludvig Holberg: *Sravnenie zhitija i del raznykh, a osoblivo vostochnykh i indijskikh, velikikh geroev i znamenitykh muzhej, po primeru Plutarkhovu.* Included among the illustrious pairs of heroes who are compared, in the manner of Plutarch's *Parallel Lives,* are Akbar, the Mughal Emperor, and Peter the Great.

Sanskrit makes an unusual appearance in an eighteenth-century utopia (not published, however, until the end of the nineteenth century). This is Prince Mikhail Shcherbatov's *Puteshestvie v zemlju Ofirskuju* (1784).[19] The author (better known for his long essay, "O povrezhdenii nravov v Rossii", 1787) of this utopian romance devotes the second chapter to providing a background for the narrator, Mr. S., a Swedish nobleman who enters the French service and is sent to India where he learns Sanskrit. This enables him, when, on returning to Europe, his ship is blown off course and he puts in to the mysterious Land of Ophir for repairs, to communicate with the remarkable natives of the utopia, since their language turns out to be Sanskrit.[20] The reference to Sanskrit in this context is quite unusual, since in a number of utopian works of the eighteenth century where attention is paid to linguistic matters the speech of the inhabitants is rather associated, explicitly or implicitly, with the Chinese language.[21]

Indian motifs also occur in eighteenth-century Russian opera. For example, the Italian composer Francesco Araja (1700-1770), who came to Russia in 1732 on an invitation from the Empress Anna Ioanovna, composed a number of operas, including *Alessandro nelle Indie* which was staged in 1755. And in 1767 Gluck's *Alessandro,* a ballet-pantomime, was produced in Russia.[22] As we shall see, Indian themes continued to appear in Russian opera, ballet, and music in the following two centuries.

We should not forget, finally, that it was during the latter part of the eighteenth century that Gerasim Lebedev was in India; some of the details of his stay there and of his accomplishments were recounted earlier in the final section of Chapter I.

CHAPTER IV

THE NINETEENTH CENTURY

I

Though we note a certain dearth of specifically oriental—including Indian—motifs in the Russian prose fiction of the early nineteenth century,[1] the literature of this century as a whole is rich in references to India. The increasing frequency of allusions to India that one encounters in both Russian prose and poetry as the century progresses is due primarily to the increased awareness of India—its cultures, languages, and literatures—on the part of the Russian reading public and Russian writers in particular. This awareness is the result in turn of increased commercial contacts with India, especially after the middle of the century,[2] as well as the rise, as noted earlier, of indological and Sanskrit studies throughout Europe and the concomitant proliferation of both scholarly and popular works dealing with these areas. For example, among the books in Pushkin's library concerned with India we find such titles as *Sacontala, ou l'Anneau fatal* (Paris, 1803), *Chefs d'oeuvre du théâtre indien* (Paris, 1828), and F.G. Eichoff's *Parallèle des langues de l'Europe et de l'Inde* (Paris, 1836). We must also, with respect especially to the period of Russian Romanticism (c. 1800-1840), take into account the significant appeal which oriental matter in general has for the romantic artist (see Friedrich Schlegel's pertinent remark quoted in the Preface to this book).

One can get a very good idea of the veritable explosion of books concerned with India published in just the first half of the century in Russia by looking at the entries in a standard bibliography such as the *Bibliografija Indii*. These cover a surprisingly wide range of areas, including literature, folklore, art and architecture, music, medicine, mathematics, education, philosophy and religion, philology, languages, dictionaries, history, geography, and travel. Of the literary works, some are translations from the French, such as *Gata-Karparam* [i.e., *Ghaṭa-karpara*], *Razgovornaja idillija* (1826), translated from A.L. de Chézy's French version. Others were translated directly into Russian from Sanskrit—e.g., *Sundas i Upasundas* (i.e., the *Sundopasunda* episode from the *Mahābhārata*), translated by K. Kossovich and published in *Moskvitjanin* (No. 2, 1844). Still others were translated from Sanskrit into German—e.g., *Vikramorwaci* [*Vikramorvaśīya*], *das ist Urwasi, der Preis der Tapferkeit, ein Drama Kālidāsa's in fünf Akten*, translated by F. Bellensen (St. Petersburg, 1846).

There are also many articles and books on the Sanskrit language, such as B. Dorn, *De affinitate linguae slavicae et sanscritae* (Khar'kov, 1833) and P. Petrov, "O svojstvakh i sostave sanskritkogo jazyka" (*Zhurnal Ministerstva narodnogo prosveshchenija*, No. 3, 1842), as well as quite scholarly editions, e.g., *Hemak'andra's Abhida nak'intamani* [i.e., Hemacandra's *Abhidhānacintāmaṇi*], *ein systematisch angeordnetes synonymisches Lexicon*, edited by O. Betlingk and Ch. Rieu (St. Petersburg, 1847).

But perhaps most interesting of all are the numerous Russian translations of fables and tales from various Indian sources noted in the *Bibliografija Indii*. These entries begin with *Istina. Indijskaja skazka* (in *Vestnik Evropy*, No. 2, 1802) and they continue throughout the century. That the listing is incomplete, however, is indicated by the fact that in the present author's possession is a copy of *Vestnik Evropy* (No. 22, 1805) beginning with a *Vostochnaja povest'* entitled *Nurmagala* which is not included in the *Bibliografija*. This is a translation from the French of Mme de Genlis' *Nourmahal ou le Règne de vingt-quatre heures* (1802). The titles of several of the tales, almost all of which are translations from the French, indicate the source—usually the *Pañcatantra*—e.g., *Ptitsa Titiba i More. Indijskaja basnja iz Panchatantry* (in *Aziatskij Vestnik*, 1826); this is the story known as "The Strandbirds and the Sea" or "The Story of the Tittibha Birds and the Sea". Occasionally the Indian tale reached Russia via a Persian collection, as in the case of *Bramin, prevrativshijsja v zoloto* (in *Vestnik Evropy*, No. 19, 1825), translated by N. Konoplev from the *Tūtīnāma* ("Parrot Book"), which is itself a Persian version of the Sanskrit *Śukasaptati* or "seventy tales of the parrot".[3]

2

During the first quarter of the nineteenth century a number of names are especially prominent in connection with Asia; and, although these are not the names of literary figures, some brief comments should be made here concerning them. The first is that of Count Sergej Uvarov (1786-1855) who became president of the Imperial Academy of Sciences in 1818 and who was later minister of education. Uvarov's early enthusiasm for oriental studies and his belief that it was somehow Russia's duty to play a leading role in the furtherance of these studies led him, in 1810, to submit a proposal for a *Projet d'une académie asiatique* (it was never implemented) which began as follows:

> There occurred during the last years of the eighteenth century a great revolution in all our ideas concerning the history of human civilization. The Orient, recently still abandoned to the lying tales of a few adventurers and the dusty works of a small number of scholars, has been unanimously recognized as the cradle of all civilization of the universe. The accidental causes of this rehabilitation have been the progress of the English in India, the conquest of the sacred language of the Brahmins... and the establishment of the Asiatic Society of Calcutta.[4]

Uvarov, an anti-Enlightenment spokesman, who later promulgated the principles of "Orthodoxy, Autocracy, and Nationality", goes on to speak of Russia's need to cherish her links with Asia and he suggests, with the enthusiastic abandon of a Friedrich von Schlegel, that just about everything of value among the ancients came from India. Uvarov's sentiments regarding Asia were echoed in a more militant fashion by the Moscow University professor and publicist, Mikhail Pogodin (1800-1875).[5]

A more colorful figure was Mikhail Magnitskij (1778-1855). A virulent opponent of the Enlightenment, he criticized Karamzin for the latter's statement that the Mongol hegemony had retarded Russia's development. In 1822 Magnitskij, who was rector of the University of Kazan', drew up plans for what he called an "Institute of the East"; this was to be established at Astrakhan' where Russian civil servants in training could communicate with and absorb the learning and wisdom of India.[6] Elsewhere he sees Biblical influences in Hinduism and equates Sarasvatī, a consort of Brahmā, with Sarah of the Old Testament.[7] Occasionally Uvarov, Pogodin, Magnitskij, and others are viewed as early nineteenth-century predecessors of the Eurasian movement of the twentieth century which will be referred to in the following chapter.

In the second half of the nineteenth century the publication of books and articles dealing with India (in the several categories noted at the beginning of this chapter) continued unabated. Especially prominent now were translations, in whole or in part, of the Sanskrit classics: excerpts from the *Mahābhārata* and the *Rāmāyaṇa*, the plays of Kālidāsa and Śūdraka, the poetry of Bhartṛhari, selections from the *Ṛg-Veda*, Indian legends and tales from the *Pañcatantra* and the *Hitopadeśa*, etc. There were philological and comparative studies in language and literature both of a very narrow range, such as Betlingk's "Ueber die Erweichung der Consonanten am Ende eines Wortes im Sanskrit", and of wider interest, e.g., V. Zhukovskij's "Jumor persidsko-indijskij"; and, of course, numerous reviews of scholarly works published abroad, such as "Novyj metricheskij perevod indusskikh dram", a review of Ludwig Fritze's *Indisches Theater* (vol. III, 1879).[8] Nor must we forget that very impressive work of lexical scholarship, the *St. Petersburg Lexicon*, published between 1852 and 1875.[9]

3

We have seen (Chapter I, section 4) how Sir William Jones' English translation of a Sanskrit classic, Kālidāsa's *Śakuntalā*, had, via a German version, caught the attention and elicited the admiration of Goethe. The latter's laudatory verses, "Sakontala", inspired by his reading of the play, soon became known in Russia in the early years of the nineteenth century and it was not long before Fedor Tjutchev provided a very free Russian adaptation. This was published in 1827 in *Severnaja lira* and runs as follows in translation:

SAKONTALA

The maidenly blush
  The young year gives to flowers;
The royal purple
  The ripe year gives to fruit;
What entrances and delights the eye
  Like the pearl growing in the sea;
What warms and enlivens the soul
  Like an all-powerful nectar;
All the flowers of dream's treasury,
  The full flower of creation,

And, in short, the very heaven of beauty
  Mirrored by the imagination—
All this Poetry has mixed
  In thee alone, Sakontala![10]

The Sanskrit dramatic classic itself continued to be read in Russia and, as we shall see in the following chapter, it was later presented on the stage in an adaptation by Konstantin Bal'mont. Later in the nineteenth century—in 1877—Marius Petipa created a ballet, *La Bayadère* (*Bajaderka*) based on the Kālidāsa play (music by Minkus) with a number of striking dances ("Hindu Dance", Jampé, "Dance Manu") that remained in the ballet repertory for many years (it was this ballet that brought fame to Anna Pavlova in 1902-1903).[11]

Goethe has another poem, "Der Gott und die Bajadere" (1797), the inspiration for which came from a reading of Pierre de Sonnerat's *Voyages aux Indes Orientales* (1782).[12] This poem was translated into Russian as *Magadèva i bajadera* by Konstantin Aksakov in 1838 (A.K. Tolstoj also has a version, *Bog i bajadera*). The ballad tells how a temple dancer falls in love with Mahādeva (i.e., Śiva) who comes to her in disguise. After the god's apparent death, the bayadere in grief attempts to commit suicide by suttee, throwing herself into the flames of his funeral pyre. But the god raises himself and her to heaven. Aksakov's version in English translation ends:

And she, stretching out her arms,
Rushed into the hot fire.
But out of the flaming circle
The marvelous youth rises
And bears in his arms
His charming beloved.[13]

In 1828 Friedrich Rückert published his free German version of the "Nala and Damayantī" episode, familiar to all students of Sanskrit, from the third book of the great Indian epic, the *Mahābhārata*. In Russia this attracted the attention, first, of Aleksandr Vel'tman, who published his version, translated from the German, in 1839: *Nalo, povest' Vrikhadazvy* [*Bṛhadaśva*] *rasskazannaja Bgaratu* [*Bhārata*]. Shortly thereafter vasilij Zhukovskij, in the course of the year 1841, translated—or, more precisely, adapted—into Russian the version by Rückert.[14] Zhukovskij's poem, published in 1844, is rather long, consisting of ten chapters (about seventy-five pages of text); from this I quote his version of what would be the first *śloka* or distich of the Sanskrit original:[15]

> Zhil byl v Indii tsar', po imeni Nal', Virazeny
> Sil'nago syn, obladatel' tsarstva Nishadskogo, ètot
> Nal' byl slaven delami, vo mladosti mudr, i prekrasen.

The same passage in Rückert's poem reads:

> Es war ein Fürst, mit Ruhm bekannt,
> Nala, der Sohn Wirasens genannt,
> Begabt mit jeglicher Tugend,
> Tapferkeit, Schönheit und jugend.

The Sanskrit distich reads, in a literal prose translation: "There was a king, Nala by name, the mighty son of Vīrasena,/ Endowed with excellent virtues, handsome, skilled in horses"; or, in Dean Milman's verse translation:

> Lived of yore, a Raja, Nala, Vīrasena's mighty son,
> Gifted he with choicest virtues, beauteous, skilled
> /in taming steeds.

In both the German and Russian versions the reference to Nala's skill with horses (*aśvakovida*) has been omitted, while Zhukovskij has—with considerable justification, however—interpolated from a later passage the reference to Nala's kingdom of Niṣadha. Further study and comparison of the full texts of the two versions with the text of the original Sanskrit will reveal numerous similar omissions, additions, and alterations, despite the preservation in both Rückert and Zhukovskij of the essential narrative line.[16] But the variations are no more radical than in the cases of many other translations or pseudo-translations of oriental classics into the modern European languages (Fitzgerald's *Rubaiyat of Omar Khayyam* is perhaps the most notorious example). Indeed, for many generations such classics have been read in the West in translations which are, more often than not, twice or even thrice removed (linguistically) from the original. In any case, Belinskij was delighted: he considered Zhukovskij's "Nala and Damayanti", with its "light, bright, transparent, grandiose, and captivating" hexameters, the best poetic production of the year.[17] And these "splendid blank verse episodes" (R. Poggioli) have no doubt over the years introduced many a Russian reader (including, possibly, Nikolaj Gumilev[18]) to the ancient Hindu epic and its mythology.

Zhukovskij also has a *Son mogol'tsa* (1806), based upon Lafontaine's *Le songe d'un habitant du Mogol*, as well as a *Lalla Ruk* and *Peri i Angel* (both 1821).[19] *Lalla Ruk*, in eight stanzas, was inspired by a reading of the oriental romance, *Lalla Rookh* (1817), by the Irish romantic poet, Thomas Moore, while the longer *Peri i Angel* is an adaptation of the second tale in *Lalla Rookh*. Moore's poem tells how Lalla Rookh ("Tulip Cheek"), the daughter of the Mughal Emperor, Aurangzeb, while on the way to be married to Sultan Aliris in Kashmir, is first entertained by and then falls in love with the poet Feramorz (he relates the four tales in the poem) and later discovers to her delight that Feramorz is Aliris. Pushkin, incidentally, thought little of either Moore ("this prim imitator of a deformed oriental imagination") or of what he felt to be Zhukovskij's efforts wasted on translation.

As for Pushkin, though he was not averse to utilizing on occasion oriental motifs (e.g., *Egipetskie nochi*, *Zolotoj petushok*), one gets the impression that he remained purposefully aloof from any romantic dalliance with far-eastern or Indian themes; that his predilections reached, so to speak, as far as the Middle East but no farther.[20] Although, as noted earlier, he had works in his library dealing with Indian (as well as Chinese) literature, there is hardly any mention of India or related matters in his poetry and prose fiction, aside from such a rare reference as

Sjuda zhemchug privez indeets

(EO, Excerpts from Onegin's Travels). Pushkin, however, does mention the works of other Russian writers who deal with Indian matter or themes; and the fact that he was at least acquainted with the *Rāmāyaṇa*, for example, is indicated by this excerpt from a letter of his to Chaadaev (18 Sept., 1831):

...Je suis sûr que le sentiment et la pensée se couvent à votre

> insu dans quelque profondeur de votre âme, seulemevnt, de se produire au dehors, elles ne sauraient, ensevelies [qu'elles] que probablement ils sont dans ce tas de vieilles idées d'habitude,de convenance, dont, vous avez beau dire, tout poéte est inévitablement [tout] pétri, quoiqu'il fasse; attendu, mon ami, que depuis l'indien Valmiki, le chantre du Ramayana et le grec Orphée... tout poète a été tenu jusqu' à cette heure de redire toujours la même chose, dans quelque lieu du monde qu'il eu chanté...[21]

But occasionally certain poems by Pushkin strike some readers, who happen to be acquainted with this or that aspect of Indian—especially religious—thought, as showing some recognizable Hindu or Buddhist feature. Thus one modern reader sees in *Prorok* what he considers to be a striking similarity to the Tantric doctrine of *kuṇḍalinī.*[22] But, upon close examination, the similarities are hardly apparent and, such as they are, in all likelihood are mere accidental resemblances. Another poem, *Anchar*, has something vaguely oriental about it, but attempts to determine its source have so far been unsuccessful.[23] The word *anchar* is of Javanese origin and *upas* of Malay origin; although there is a *viṣavṛkṣa* or poison tree in the Indian tradition (it occurs, e.g., in Kalhaṇa's *Rājataraṅgiṇī*), there does not seem to be any recognizable connection with Pushkin's image.

Finally, in the notes to his planned *Istorija Petra* Pushkin has the following:

> Peter stopped at Upper Volochok, examined the Tvertsa and Msta rivers and decided to connect them and thereby to join the Baltic and the Caspian; he thus discovered a route between India and Petersburg.[24]

As for the poets of the "Pushkin Pleiad", Denis Davydov (1784-1839), although references to India do not occur in his verse, had an interest in India and an MS entitled *Zamechanija ob Indii* is in his archives.[25] Dmitrij Venevitinov (1805-1827) refers to the "rose of Kashmir" in his *Tri rozy*; and Anton Del'vig in his *Na smert' sobachki Amiki* (1821) has the lines:

> The finest silk of Hindustan and Persia
> Cannot compare in lustre or in softness
> With her fluffy and curly fur.

The poet P.A. Vjazemskij has nothing of India in his verse but his son, Prince Pavel Petrovich (1820-1888), who served in the Ministry of Foreign Affairs and wrote a number of literary studies concerned especially with old Russian literature, has an entry in the *Bibliografija Indii.*[26] Evgenij Baratynskij (1800-1844) makes passing mention of Indians in his *Tsyganka* (1835):

> Like a crown around his head
> The Indian whirls his nimble knives.

One might have expected his *Pereselenie dush* to concern India, but it is actually set in ancient Egypt.

Though there is much of the East in the poetry of Mikhail Lermontov, this almost always involves the Near East and the Caucasus and Central Asia; but his long *Angel smerti* (1831), subtitled *Vostochnaja povest'*, which begins

> The golden East, land of marvels,
> Land of love and voluptuousness,

is set in India

> Beneath the hot skies of Hindustan.

We owe to the minor poet Mikhail Delarju (1811-1868) five pleasant Russian versions of selections from the *Amaruśataka* ("The Century of Amaru"), a collection of erotic poems by various Sanskrit poets of the seventh and eighth centuries. Delarju did not, of course, work from the Sanskrit but used the French prose version of de Chézy (*Anthologie érotique d'Amarou*, Paris, 1831). Here is one example of a poem (1832) by Delarju in English translation:

> This impertinent lover
> Whom I drove away in anger,
> This cruel man who thought
> Only of himself at *that* moment—
> If this treacherous one should,
> With new impertinence, return,
> Tell me, dear friend,
> What shall I do then?[27]

A closer prose version of the original Sanskrit is offered by Professor Sushīl Kumār De: "In playful anger, dear friend, I just said to my beloved: 'Depart', and straightway the hardhearted one sprang from the couch and went indeed. For that cruel one who broke off love so violently, my shameless heart yearns again,—and what can I do?"[28]

Inspired by the story of the courtesan Vasantasenā in Śūdraka's play *Mṛcchakaṭika* ("The Little Clay Cart"), Dmitrij Oznabishin (d. 1877) wrote his poem *Vazantazena* in 1832. The poor brāhmaṇa Cārudatta pursues Vasantasenā who flees, "trembling like a banana branch", but

In vain...Her purple veil
Flutters in the breeze,
The bells about her waist
And on her nimble feet tinkle;
Precious stones sparkle
In her hair and the sultry air
Stirs her young breasts,
Held firm in cups of gold.

(Russian text in *Poèty* 1820-1830-*kh godov*, Leningrad, 1972, II, pp. 88-89) Oznabishin made considerable progress in the study of Sanskrit and in 1826 published an article, "Izobrazhenie sanskritskoj literatury", in *Syn otechestva.*

Apollon Grigor'ev (1822-1864) was both poet and critic and his name is important—as that of an exponent of German organic philosophy—in connection with Dostoevskij and the later Russian symbolist movement. He has a number of poems with Indian allusions (e.g., *Predsmertnaja ispoved'*) but one of his most representative efforts in this respect is his *Molitva parii* ("The Pariah's Prayer", 1845) which is a free translation of Goethe's three-stanza *Des Paria Gebet* (1824), the first part of the trilogy, *Paria.* The source of Goethe's poem may be found in Pierre de Sonnerat's *Voyages aux Indes Orientales.*[29] I quote here the first stanza of Goethe's poem and the first of Grigor'ev's Russian version:

Grosser Brahma, Herr der Mächte!
Alles ist von deinem Samen,
Und so bist du der Gerechte!
Hast du denn allein die Brahmen,
Nur die Rajahs und die Reichen,

Hast du sie allein geschaffen?
Oder bist auch du's der affen
Werden liess und unseresgleichen?

Vechnyj Brama; bozhe slavy,
Semja ty vsemu edinyj,
I lish' ty edinyj pravyj...
Neuzhel' odni braminy
Da bogatye s radzhami
Sozdany toboju, bozhe,
Ili zveri vmeste s nami
Ruk tvoikh sozdan'e tozhe?[30]

Among the many translations from numerous literatures made by the minor radical poet Mikhail Mikhajlov (he died in Siberia in 1865) are versions of three short poems from the *Śatakatrayam*, a collection of brief lyric and gnomic poems by Bhartṛhari (7th cent. ?). Mikhajlov did not translate directly from the Sanskrit but made use of the several translations of Bhartṛhari available in modern European languages.[31] I quote here in English translation the first of three poems by Mikhajlov published in 1862:

Though the lamp burns,
Though the fire glows,
Though the moon shines
In the starry heaven,
Though the sun is bright:
If the eyes of my beloved
Do not shine on me,
The world around me
Is wrapped in darkness.

This poem by Bhartṛhari has also been translated from Sanskrit into English by Barbara Miller:

Beside a lamp or flaming hearth,
In light of stars or sun or moon,
Without her fawnlike eyes
My world remains in darkness.[32]

Mikhajlov also did a version of the fable from Pilpay entitled

Dvoe prokhozhikh i klad[33] which had earlier been translated by B. Volkov and V. Majkov.

In 1881 the minor poet Nikolaj Berg (d. 1884) published a collection of verse entitled *Srngaratilakam ili kniga ljubvi.* Though the Sanskrit of the title (*Śṛṅgāratilaka*) is the title of several actual Sanskrit works on erotic love (*Śṛṅgāra*), Berg's verses are free adaptations of the poetry of Bhartṛhari; indeed, most of the offerings are really original verses inspired by a reading of Bhartṛhari. In a letter to Berg in 1882 Ivan Turgenev writes that his verses are distinguished by "melodiousness and grandiosity of content" (*Poèty* 1840-1850-*kh godov*, Leningrad, 1972, p. 428).

Among the frequently neglected non-civic and "Parnassian" poets active towards the end of the century prior to the appearance of the decadents and symbolists, several were attracted by Indian motifs. Count P. Buturlin (d. 1895), for example, has a long poem of ten stanzas entitled *Bajadera* (1888) in which a bayadere looks forward, through the emptiness of her life, to utter extinction or nirvāṇa:

> Here days without mirth, here nights without feasts,
> Here thought does not tire nor pleasures pall,
> In Nirvāṇa all shame will vanish and love as well...

Dmitrij Tsertelev (d. 1911), an admirer of Schopenhauer, has a *Zhertovoprinoshenie Buddy* (1892) about the child Buddha making an offering in a temple; the poem contains a number of references to India (Varuna, Chandra, Suriya, Brahma, Prajapati). Count Arsenij Golenishchev-Kutuzov (d. 1912), who is perhaps best known for his "Songs and Dances of Death" set to music by his friend Musorgskij, is occasionally called the "poet of Nirvana", not because of any preoccupation with this concept but simply because of his predilection for the themes of death, oblivion, and extinction.

A more familiar name is that of Semen Nadson (d. 1887), a poet of partly Jewish descent who died at the very young age of twenty-five. His verse was once immensely popular but is now rated quite modestly (indeed, Mirsky calls it the "low-water mark of Russian poetical taste"). Nadson was also attracted by Indian legends, especially those associated with Buddha, and his *Tri nochi Buddy* (1885), which exists in two inchoate versions, gives us again an idealized picture (the "blue Ganges"!) of the Buddha's birthplace (Kapilavastu)

> In a land where the sun spares
> Neither its heat nor its bright rays,
> Where the blue Ganges flows peacefully
> Amidst the quiet fields of rice,
> Where the Himalayan peaks,
> Above the valley's motley floor,
> Glow with their eternal snow...
> We see a distant city,
> The capital of this sultry land—Kapilavastu.

(Poems involving Indian themes by Bal'mont, Brjusov, and Merezhkovskij written towards the end of the nineteenth century will be mentioned in the following chapter.)

4

In Russian prose, despite the overall scarcity of oriental tales specifically involving India in the early 1800's, we do find occasional examples. Thus very early in the century (1809) Aleksandr Benitskij published in the short-lived periodical *Tsvetnik* an *Indijskaja skazka* entitled *Na drugoi den'*.[34] The story is a simple one: Narud, the governor of an Indian province, falls in love with Onida, the daughter of a poor soldier, whom he visits disguised as a merchant; she tells Narud that her father, wounded in battle, had long but in vain sought a pension from Narud's corrupt subordinates; Narud, the model of a just and virtuous ruler, removes these officials and corrects the situation. There is little else in the story that is specifically Indian or, for that matter, Asiatic—even the names are nondescript and only sound vaguely oriental. Benitskij also has a poem entitled "The Return of Bacchus from India" (1809); this is not drawn, however, from the author's own knowledge of the legend, mentioned at the beginning of Chapter I, concerning Dionysus in India but is simply a loose translation of a much better poem by the minor German poet J.G. Willamov.

V.F. Odoevskij's "Indian Tale", *Pereplava*, appeared in the *Moskovskij vestnik* in 1827. An adaptation from the French, it elicited the following remark from Pushkin (in a letter to M. Pogodin, 31 August, 1827): "Your Indian tale, 'The Crossing', would attract general attention in a European journal as a curious disclosure of learning, but here with us they see only a tale and they solemnly find it stupid".[35] Odoevskij also makes a brief reference to India in his *Russkie nochi* ("Second Night").

In the case of Belinskij, mentioned in the previous section in connection with Zhukovskij, it might be noted here that he translated into Russian an article by an unknown author which appeared in the journal *Molva* in 1833; this was "Den' v Kal'kutte" which deals with the greed and the pettiness of the British in Calcutta. Belinskij also reacted favorably to an article on Hindu mythology ("Verovanija indusov") which appeared in *Otechestvennye zapiski* in 1845 (No. 11). But the notorious Faddej Bulgarin was shocked and wrote a letter of denunciation to General Du'bel't in the Third Section. Nothing points up better the type of character Bulgarin was than this letter, entitled "Sotsialism i Komunism, Panteism v Rossii za poslednee 25-letie". In the letter Bulgarin states that the purpose of the article obviously was to insinuate that the story of Jesus was derived from the Hindu myth of Kṛṣṇa, that this insinuation was emphasized by the periodical's pointing out that the celebration of Kṛṣṇa's birth occurred on 24/25 December, etc., etc.[36]

But comments on India occur more frequently in the writings of the Civic critics, N.G. Chernyshevskij and N.A. Dobroljubov. In his review of G.T. Buckle's *History of Civilisation in England* (1857), Chernyshevskij mentions the achievements of the Hindus in medicine and mathematics and criticizes Buckle for under-estimating these achievements.[37] So, too, in his review of a German scholar's survey of world poetry he criticizes the author for not even mentioning the Vedas.[38] Chernyshevskij was also bold enough to review two studies by the Russian scholar, A. Gil'ferding, *O srodstve jazyka slavjanskogo s sanskritskim* (St. Petersburg, 1853) and *Ob otnoshenii jazyka slavjanskogo k jazykam rodstvennym* (Moscow, 1853).[39] Although Chernyshevskij was trained as a philologist, his reviews are mediocre and rather pitiful; in any case, his utilitarian views and his more practical concerns later caused him to speak with scorn about the uselessness of Sanskrit (which he did not know) or, for that matter, about the ability to distinguish between big and little *jus*.[40]

In one of his best-known essays, "Russkij chelovek na rendezvous" (1858), Chernyshevskij writes that those who come to believe that all people are really alike will find the peace of mind of the Brāhmaṇa contemplating his navel and repeating 'Om mani padme kum". But *Om maṇi padme hūṃ* is the Buddhist *vidyā ṣaḍakṣarī* or mystical formulary and its incongruous association with a Brāhmaṇa reminds one, unfortunately, of Chernyshevskij's confusing such things as Madeira and beer.[41]

Dobroljubov's interest in India is shown by his essay, "Vzgljad na istoriju i sovremennoe sostojanie Ost-Indii", which appeared in *Sovremennik*, No. 9, 1857. In this article, written at the time of the Mutiny,[42] Dobroljubov traces the history of India, especially under the Mughals and the British; he cites the caste system and the Indian counterpart of the *obshchina* as impediments to social progress and he condemns, as the British themselves did, the religious cults of Hinduism:

> Religious formalism produced an absurd group of fakirs with innumerable ugly varieties, while the desolate vegetable existence of the Indians was made even more miserable by the baleful influence of the Brahmans.

But, *mutatis mutandis*, the same—or worse—might be said of Russia in the 1850's.

Aleksandr Ostrovskij (1823-1886), the most prolific of the Russian dramatists, whose plays have long provided a staple repertory for the Russian stage, hardly strikes one familiar with his works as a writer likely to have translated, via a French version, an obscure play originally written in Tamil. But in 1923 it was decided, in connection with the centenary of Ostrovskij's birth, to publish certain material by the dramatist preserved in the *Pushkinskij dom*; among this material was a short comedy in four parts (or scenes) entitled *Dèvadassi* and bearing the following note by Ostrovskij:

> A translation of this play from the "Tamoul" Indian dialect (a southern dialect, very close to Sanskrit) into French is found in the book, *Les moeurs et les femmes de l'extrême orient. Voyage au pays des perles, par Louis Jacolliot*. Paris, 1874.[43]

The Russian Indologist, S.F. Ol'denburg, in his brief introduction to *Dévadassi*, points out that Tamil is not at all, as Ostrovskij writes, related to Sanskrit (it is not Indo-European); that Jacolliot elsewhere refers to the author of the play as "Parasuram", an otherwise unknown actor and writer who flourished in the forties of the nineteenth century (and who might have lived in the vicinity of Pondichéry[44]); that the Tamil original is not extant; and that the comedy is a rather ordinary one.

The title, *Dèvadassi*, is the Sanskrit word *devadāsī* which means a temple prostitute and dancing girl, or bayadere, and the plot is a simple one. Rangassami, a traveling musician, contrives with Lachumiama, an old bayadere, to cause Anniama, the daughter of a market woman, to give herself to a rich young merchant, Saverinaden. They succeed, but Saverinaden then repudiates Anniama and her child. Anniama goes to court to seek justice, asking for witnesses (here the text of Ostrovskij's translation ends); but everyone rejects her. Saverinaden, however, feels sorry for her, acknowledges her as his wife and the child as his; the crowd deals with Rangassami and the court punishes Lachumiama.

The language of the play is a strange mixture, combining words like *siesta*, *kuli*, and *konfeti* with less familiar words such as *ikhnevmon*, *gaudag* (i.e., howdah), *amrita* (ambrosia), and *kallju* (fermented cocoanut milk).

Incidentally, several of Jacolliot's works had earlier been excerpted and translated into Russian. These include *Strana zhemchuga* (*Pays des perles*, 1874) and *Tri mesjatsa na Gange* (*Trois mois sur le Gange et le Brahmapoutra* by Mme de Jacolliot, Paris, 1875), published in *Vsemirnyj puteshestvennik*, numbers 7 and 8, 1876, and *Spiritizm v Indii. Fakiry-ocharovateli* (*Le Spiritisme dans le monde. L'initiation et les sciences occultes dans l'Inde*, Paris, 1875), St. Petersburg, 1883.

5

The connections and associations between Lev Tolstoj (1828-1910) and India, not to mention the Orient in general,[45] are numerous; but they either almost wholly involve non-literary matters or pertain to certain aspects of Tolstoj's nature or creativity which have elicited from others remarks concerning India, Hinduism, or Buddhism.[46] Belonging to the former category are, for example, the well-known connections between Tolstoj and Gāndhī; belonging to the latter are such statements as those made concerning Tolstoj by Melchior de Vogüé in his *Le roman russe*. Here, however, I shall first quote some interesting passages from de Vogüé's book concerning certain supposed similarities between Indians and Russians and, in the following chapter, mention the associations between Tolstoj and Gāndhī.

Eugène Melchior Vicomte de Vogüé (1848-1910) was a French writer and critic who, during his seven years of service in Russia as secretary of the French embassy in St. Petersburg, learned Russian and became greatly interested in Russian literature. His *Le roman russe*, which appeared in 1886, was instrumental in stimulating, in France and elsewhere, an interest in the Russian novel, especially in the works of Tolstoj and Dostoevskij. The French critic begins his study with a discourse on the Slavic background and on what we might call certain ethnico-spiritual affiliations in quaint but unabashedly bold terms:

> On découvre dans le cas du peuple russe une peine historique: elle provient en partie d'un mal héréditaire, du aux premiers ancêtres, en partie de maux contractés durant la suite de l'existence. Le mal héréditaire, gardé des plus lointaines origines, c'est le penchant de l'esprit slave vers cette doctrine négative que nous appelons aujourd'hui le nihilisme et qui s'est appelée du même nom chez les péres hindous, le *nirvana*. Si l'on veut bien connaître la Russie, il faut se remémorer tout ce que l'on a appris de l'Inde ancienne.[47]

The French reader, he adds, might certainly regard these remarks as novel (as we assuredly do today):

> Cette vue paraitra peut-être un peu trop nouvelle au lecteur français pour qu'il l'accepte; elle est familière au monde savant en Russie, où quelques philosophes se réclament directement de la doctrine du Bouddha et vantent avec fierté la pureté de leur sang aryen. Il n'est pas rare d'entendre un savant de ce pays dire à un étranger avec une certaine présomption: "Vous ne comprendrez jamais comme nous l'esprit des vieux Aryas; vous n'êtes que leurs neveux éloignés: nous sommes leur lignée immédiate".

De Vogüé then adduces what he considers evidence:

> Ceux qui parlent ainsi ne manquent pas d'arguments à l'appui de leur thèse. Ils ont d'abord le type physique, resté si pur

dans les familles qui ne sont pas melangées de sang tartare; tel étudiant de Moscou, tel paysan de certaines provinces pourraient passer dans une rue de Lahore ou de Bénarès, sans que rien les distinguât, sauf le teint, des indigènes de la vallée du Gange.

But he is on slightly safer ground when he talks philology:

> Ils ont surtout des raisons philologiques de premier ordre. Si l'on classe les langues indoeuropéennes d'après leur ordre de parenté avec le sanscrit, les idiomes slaves occuperont une place à part, plus rapprochée que les autres de la langue mère, ou de la langue soeur. Les tables comparatives dressées par les linguistes qui font autorité dans ces questions accusent un parallélisme plus étroit entre le vieux slavon et le sanscrit, qu'entre cette dernière langue et le grec des plus anciennes époques... Nommez à un paysan russe le Véda, il comprendra sans plus d'explications: le verbe *védat* est un des plus usuels de son parler.

He then goes on to associate the terms "nihilism" and *nirvāṇa:*

> Comme le christianisme pour l'Occident, le bouddhisme fut pour l'extrême Orient la révélation de charité, de douceur, de liberté morale et sociale qui devait rendre la vie plus supportable à des multitudes d'êtres humains, courbés sous le joug d'une théocratie implacable. Les meilleures doctrines doivent comporter, pour réussir, certaines exagérations qui répondent aux prédispositions maladives des races; elles doivent tolérer certaines erreurs qui séduisent les imaginations faussées par de longues souffrances. À ces dernières, le christianisme offrit l'ascétisme; le bouddhisme leur ménagea les joies de l'anéantissement, le *nirvana.* C'est pour traduire ce mot que celui de *nihilisme* a été, si je ne me trompe, inventé par Bournouf. Si vous voulez une définition plus précise du *nirvana,* Max Müller vous dira que le vocable sanscrit signifie proprement: "L'action d'éteindre une lumière en la soufflant". Cette définition ne convient-elle pas au nihilisme russe? N'est-ce pas la lumière de la civilisation qu'il veut souffler, pour se réplonger dans le néant?

De Vogüé is correct, in the last paragraph, with respect both to Max Müller's definition and to the French orientalist, Eugène

Burnouf's use of *nihilisme* to render the Sanskrit word *nirvāṇa* (in his *Introduction à l'histoire du Bouddhisme indien*, 1844), but in error about Burnouf's having coined the word.[48] And for de Vogüé to equate the two terms, either as words or as concepts, is quite absurd.

Later (in Chapter VI of his book) de Vogüé, in attempting to sum up, as many critics have tried to do, the two "faces" of Tolstoj, writes: "On dirait l'esprit d'un chimiste anglais dans l'ame d'un bouddhiste hindou". This is one of de Vogüé's best known comments on Tolstoj and it is quoted with relish by the American critic, James Gibbons Huneker, in *Ivory, Apes, and Peacocks* (Chapter IV).[49]

It is remarkable that Konstantin Leont'ev, in his *Analiz, stil' i vejanie. O romanakh gr. L. N. Tolstogo* (1890), should also have turned to India in searching for the proper metaphor with which to describe *War and Peace*:

> When, according to P. Boborykin, Turgenev so nobly and judiciously said that his own talent could not be compared to Tolstoy's, and that "Lyovushka Tolstoy is an elephant", it seems to me that he was at that moment thinking particularly of *War and Peace*. It is indeed an elephant! Or, if you wish something more monstrous, it is an excavated Sivatherium in the flesh—the Sivatherium, whose huge skulls are kept in India in temples of the god Shiva. The trunk, the huge body, the tusks (besides tusks, there are also horns) all run contrary to every zoological rule of propriety.[50]

In compiling his *Azbuka* (Primer) during 1871-1872, along with fables and folktales from Greek, Jewish, and Oriental sources, Tolstoj included material of Indian origin.[51] In the *Azbuka*, published in 1872, Tolstoj attempted with perverse ingenuity to put into practice his pedagogical theories; but the primer was ill received and severely criticized. The *Novaja azbuka*, published in 1874-1875, was more successful, since Strakhov had meanwhile prevailed upon Nekrasov to publish Tolstoj's writings on pedagogy in *Otechestvennye zapiski*. The four *Russkie knigi dlja chtenija* (1875) also contain material of ultimately Indian origin. Thus in the first book there are several stories, some abbreviated and reworked, translated from *Les avadanas, contes et apologues in-*

diens (Paris, 1859)[52]—e.g., *Golova i khvost zmei* and *Delezh nasledstva*—as well as from a French version of a Persian translation of the "Fables of Bidpai" (e.g., *Obez'jana*).

Several years ago a book appeared, entitled *Karma/Nirvana: Two Buddhist Tales*, by Paul Carus, with a Preface by Leo Tolstoj.[53] This was a new edition of *Karma*, with the addition of *Nirvana*, which first appeared in *The Open Court* magazine (Chicago) in 1894. Paul Carus (1852-1919) was a German-born American editor and philosopher who was particularly interested in the Oriental religions, especially Buddhism; he edited the journals *The Open Court* and *The Monist* in Chicago and directed the Open Court Publishing Company which specialized, as it still does, in books on philosophy, religion, and literature. Lev Tolstoj made a Russian translation of Carus' tale which was published in *Severnyj vestnik* (No. 12, 1894'.)[54] Tolstoj's Russian version was translated into French by E. Halpérine-Kaminsky and published as a work by Tolstoj under the title *Imitations* in Paris in 1900. From this a German translation was made of the story, which still carried Tolstoj's name as the author, and later an English translation was published in Chicago. Paul Carus wrote Tolstoj and explained the situation and Tolstoj in turn expressed his regrets.[55]

6

When we turn from Tolstoj to Dostoevskij and Turgenev and look for references to India or Indian motifs and imagery, we find nothing. Occasionally, however, scholars might note certain aspects of Dostoevskij's philosophy which seem to suggest the Orient (aside, that is, from the familiar "Chinese Mandarin" story[56]); thus Irene Kirk has pointed out what may be interpreted as Buddhistic elements in *The Idiot* as well as certain similarities between Prince Myshkin and Gautama Buddha.[57] And anyone familiar with Vedic and Sanskrit literature might well recall, in connection with Dostoevskij, the plot of the *Mahābhārata* and the "Gambler's Lament" in the *Ṛg-Veda*. As for Turgenev, about all we can say is that he once stayed with Professor Max Müller, the Vedic and Sanskrit scholar, at Oxford in 1878 and that A.F. Koni in his *Pamjati Turgeneva*, taking *tat tvam asi* to mean "This is also you", applies it to Turgenev, able as a writer to put himself in another's place.

In the stories and plays of Anton Chekhov (1860-1904), whose name is often mentioned in connection with Tolstoj,[58] there are hardly any references to India (aside from the passing mention of gypsies in India in *Zheny artistov* and of Buddha in *Chernyj monakh*). But in 1890 Chekhov paid a brief visit to India and Ceylon, as well as China and Japan, and he seems to have made love with an Indian girl on the latter island.[59] Some years later, in a letter to Suvorin (1897), Chekhov refers to his fellow Russian physician, Vladimir Aaronovich Khavkin (1860-1930). Khavkin graduated from Odessa University and went to India in 1893 where he remained until 1915. As an epidemiologist, Khavkin worked in Bombay to control cholera and bubonic plague. An institute, the "Haffkine Institute", was later established in his honor in Bombay and is still functioning today. In another letter to Suvorin (1899) Chekhov writes more on Khavkin:

> ...we are indebted to a Russian doctor by the name of Khavkin, a Jew. In Russia he is completely unknown, though in England he has long been hailed as a great philanthropist. The life story of this Jew, so detested by the Hindus, who almost killed him, is indeed remarkable.[60]

Another major nineteenth-century Russian novelist, Ivan Goncharov (1812-1891), although he refers in *Oblomov* (1859) to the Asiatic aspects of Oblomov's dressing-gown (*khalat*), does not mention India.[61] Nor did his extensive sea-voyage, of which he has left us an account in his *Fregat Pallada* (1856), bring him to India (he visited Africa, China, Japan, the Philippines, and Java).[62] But he did dream about India and he gave vent to his romantic aspirations in the following passage:

> I want to go to Brazil, to India; I want to go where the sun calls forth life from stone and nearby transforms all that it touches with its fire back into stone; where, like our forefathers, man reaps unsown fruit, where the lion roars, the serpent creeps, where eternal summer rules—there, to the bright temples of God's world, where nature, like a bayadere, breathes sensuality, where it is sultry, terrifying and fascinating to live, where the enfeebled imagination grows numb before a finished creation, where one's eyes will not weary of gazing, and the heart throbs.[63]

The minor but once very popular novelist, G.P. Danilevskij

(1829-1890), has an historical novel entitled *To India Under Peter the First* ("Na Indiju pri Petre Pervom", 1879),[64] based upon some of the fact and fancy surrounding Peter the Great's rather vague intentions, early in the eighteenth century, to send a Russian military detachment to India, ostensibly for the purpose of establishing trade relations. The novel is very dull but this dullness is offset to some extent by the novel's brevity—a brevity that was, so to speak, predetermined, since Peter's Indian campaign was never in fact realized.

We might mention also that the eminent Ukrainian writer, Ivan Franko (1856-1916), in addition to his novels, short stories, and poems, did some translations of Indian material, mostly from earlier German versions. Among his collected works there are, for example, the *Indijs'ki legendy*, consisting of "Manu i potop svitu" and "Sund i Upasund". Both verse excerpts are from the *Mahābhārata*: the former is the story of Manu and the Flood, the latter the story of Sunda and Upasunda.[65] The dramatic poem *Tsar i Asket* (1892) is a free adaptation based upon an excerpt from the *Mārkaṇḍeya Purāṇa* which Franko read in a translation by Friedrich Rückert. Franko also supplies a brief survey of Sanskrit literature (also based on German sources) as well as a commentary on the story of King Hariścandra (the *tsar*) and the Ṛṣi Viśvāmitra (the *asket*).[66]

7

It is natural that the so-called Russian philosophers and religious thinkers of the nineteenth century should have touched upon some aspects of India in their writings. Here I shall mention only a few examples, beginning with Peter Chaadaev (1793-1856). Chaadaev refers to India in his *Letters* (6 & 7), and in his *Apologie d'un fou* he writes: "We are simply a nation of the North, and in our ideas as well as our climate far removed from the scented Vale of Kashmir and the holy shores of the Ganges".[67] Aleksej Khomjakov (1804-1860), who compiled a dictionary of Russian words akin to Sanskrit (*Sravnenie russkikh slov s sanskritskimi*[68]), also refers to various features of Hinduism and Buddhism in his works.[69] But the most significant figure is that of Vladimir Solov'ev (1853-1900), who is especially important in connection with the "second wave" of Russian symbolist poets to be mentioned in the following chapter. Solov'ev's religious and mystical concepts draw upon a wide range of both occidental and oriental thought; and we find in his prose and poetry Indian—especially Buddhist—imagery and allusions. An example from his verse would be *Ex Oriente Lux* (1890) which combines Indian and classical Greek allusions; the third stanza reads:

> And who passed the road of glory
> To India and the Ganges?
> The Macedonian phalanx,
> The imperial eagles of Rome.

Even in his *misterija-shutka, Belaja lilija ili son v noch' Pokrova* (1893), Solov'ev has a character, "Nepljuj-na-stol", a *drevnij mudrets*, who says, for example,

> Then from Kuku-nor through Kaluga
> I walked so as to find
> Him whose name in Kashmir,
> In all Tibet, the Pamirs,
> Is quite well known to all...

And it is in his philosophical and religious writings that we find a brief, but careful and sympathetic, consideration of Hindu and Buddhist religious concepts. Thus in the second chapter of *The Justification of the Good* (*Opravdanie dobra: nravstvennaja filosofija*)[70] Solov'ev discusses the ascetic principle in morality and considers, in this light, two of the major Hindu systems, Vedānta and Sāṃkhya, as well as Buddhism. He refers with what appears to be a clear understanding to such terms and concepts as *paramātman* (supreme spirit), *puruṣa* (soul or spirit), *prakṛti* (primary substance), and *advaita* (monism). Solov'ev devotes more attention to Buddhism (pp. 228-236) but criticizes it from the Christian point of view as morally inconsistent (much as a Buddhist might criticize Christian doctrine). To make a point, he tells the story of Āryadeva (a pupil of the early Buddhist teacher, Nāgārjuna), the wounded dog, and the worms; this incident (or apologue) is similar to the one used by Merezhkovskij in his poem, *Zhertva* (see below, Chapter V). Nevertheless, Solov'ev pays homage to Buddhism in the following terms:

> The negative infinity of human personality had been apparent

> to individual philosophers before the time of Buddhism. But it was in Buddhism that this view found its first historical expression in the collective life of humanity. Owing to his morally-practical universalism which proceeded from the heart even more than from the mind, Buddha Śākyamuni created a form of common life hitherto unknown in humanity—the brotherhood of beggar-monks from every caste and nation—the "listeners" (Shravaki) of the true doctrine, the followers of the true way. Here for the first time the worth of the individual and his relation to society were finally determined not by the *fact* of being born into a certain class or a definite national and political organization, but by the inner *act* of choosing a certain moral ideal (p. 229).

It is noteworthy that Henri de Lubac quotes this passage from Solov'ev in his study, *La rencontre du bouddhisme et l'occident.*[71]

8

As for India and the other arts in Russia, Petipa's ballet *La Bayadère*, which premiered in 1877, retained its popularity. The Belgian choreographer, Joseph Hansen, produced his first ballet in Moscow, *La Fille d'Inferno*, in November, 1879; the story here is laid in India. Joseph Mendes (Mendez), of Spanish origin, became ballet-master at the Bol'shoj in 1889 and in February of 1890 he staged his *India*, an exotic *ballet-féerie*. Mendes' sister-in-law, Adelina Giuri, one of the most elegant ballerinas in Moscow towards the end of the century, displayed her technical skill especially well as Padmana in Ippolito Monplaisir's *Bramah* in 1897.[72] In the case of opera, one of Fedor Chaliapin's notable roles was that of the priest Nīlakaṇṭha in Delibes' *Lakmé*, set in India, which was staged in Moscow in 1896.[73]

The Russian painter, V.V. Vereshchagin (1842-1904), visited India twice in the seventies and eighties. On the basis of sketches made during these visits, Vereshchagin produced thirty-six paintings.[74] Six of these in the "Indian series" are reproduced in black and white in an English translation of Ivan Minaev's *Ocherki Tsejlona i Indii* printed in India.[75] Vereshchagin was disturbed by the actions of the British in India and one of his best-known paintings, especially in the Soviet Union, is *Anglijskaja kazn' v Indii.*

A less famous Russian artist associated with India was Prince

A.D. Saltykov who toured India between 1841 and 1845. Saltykov has left us his impressions of India both in his *Pis'ma ob Indii*, first serialized and later published in Moscow in 1851, and in a series of sketches, four of which are also reproduced in the work by Minaev cited above.[76] Saltykov's *Letters* appeared in a French translation (*Lettres sur l'Inde*, Paris, 1848) which came to the attention of Karl Marx. His sketches were also published in Paris in 1853 (*Habitants de l'Inde dessinés d'après nature par le prince A. Soltykoff*).

We might mention here two matters of special interest noted by Ljusternik in his *Russko-indijskie èkonomicheskie, nauchnye i kul' turnye svjazi XIX v.* One of these concerns a work published, it appears, in Calcutta (but *sine loco, sine anno*) sometime in the sixties by an English missionary, the Rev. James Long; this was his *Village Communities in India and Russia*, a study and comparison of certain features of the reforms of the sixties in Russia pertaining to land and village communities, and the land situation and similar communities in India following the Mutiny of 1857. The Rev. Long, who seems also to have visited Russia, gives a detailed explanation of such terms as *mir, artel'*, and *starosta*.

The other matter is the inauguration of the first regular Odessa-Bombay steamship passage. This occurred on 12 February, 1871, when the steamship *Nakhimov* sailed from Odessa. The ship, under Capt. P.K. Grekke, passed through the Suez Canal and reached Bombay on 12 March; she sailed again on 23 March, returning to Odessa on 19 April.

I shall close this chapter with some brief remarks concerning the Gypsy language (*romani*), which bears a close resemblance in several respects to the Indo-European languages of India. This close relationship can clearly be seen if one compares, for example, the names of the *romani* numbers from one to ten with those of Hindi,[77] while in the titles of some Gypsy songs, e.g., *Kamau tut* ("I love you"), we can often see further close resemblances to the Indian languages. It is interesting that a *romani* word for the Christian cross, *trishul*, is the equivalent of the Sanskrit *triśūla* (trident of Śiva) and that a number of *romani* words, all with Indic cognates, are found in Russian, especially in the jargons. For instance, *raklo*, "small-time crook" (cf. Gypsy *raklo*, "youth"), is cited by Galler and Marquess in *Soviet Prison Camp Speech*.[78]

CHAPTER V

THE TWENTIETH CENTURY

1

The Silver Age of Russian literature (or, as it is occasionally called, Russian Modernism or Symbolism), which actually began about two decades before the end of the nineteenth century, was essentially a neoromantic movement and, as such, showed a marked interest in the exoticism of the Orient, including India. Before the Modernist movement had run its full course, however, and after Symbolism was succeeded by Acmeism and Futurism, the Russian Revolution of 1917 interrupted the normal course of development. Though many of the modernist, symbolist, and futurist tendencies persisted after 1917, by 1932, when the Soviet government turned its official attention to literature and the other arts, such modernizing movements, profoundly influenced by Western thought and sensibilities, were brought rather abruptly to an end, at least so far as "socialist realist" literature was concerned. But the romantic interest in the Orient on the part of the symbolists was replaced, to some extent, by the "internationalist" tendencies of Russian Communism; these tendencies (most often, to be sure, capricious, deceptive, and sentimental) resulted in lines such as the following (from Irakli Abashidze's *Poètam Indii*):

> While the moon pours its rays,
> Evanescent and weightless,
> Flaming words will sing praise
> To new India's greatness.
> We shall sing of the charms
> Of the Indian maid
> And the velvety arms
> That my fancy invade.
> Kindling friendship in souls
> From Tbilisi and Delhi,
> Hindi verses will blend
> With the rhythms of Khartveli.[1]

There was, towards the end of the nineteenth and into the twentieth century, a tremendous increase in the number of books, articles, and other publications concerned with various aspects of India as well as with the relations between India and Russia (or the Soviet Union). It would be a vain endeavor even merely to list representative works; an idea of the bulk of the material can only be had if one surveys the entries in the latest edition of the *Bibliografija Indii*. There was of course a very great increase—as compared with the nineteenth century—in the number of translations from Sanskrit, Pali, and the modern languages and literatures of India and an even greater number of publications in the fields of history, economics, politics, and diplomacy. The great mass of published material on India that had accumulated during the nineteenth century and continued to accumulate during the first half of the twentieth century resulted almost naturally in the fact that more and more of this information found its way into literature. Wolfgang Reif, for example, writes the following in this connection:

> Nachdem die wichtigsten indischen und chinesischen Dichtungen und religiösen Texte in Uebersetzungen vorlagen, setzte etwa um die Jahrhundertwende eine verstärkte Rezeption östlicher Kultur ein, welche sich zu einem entscheidenden Faktor des europäischen Geisteslebens auswuchs.[2]

In the nineties of the preceding century some of those poets who became involved, largely under the influence of French symbolism, in the early phase of Russian modernism or neoromanticism were attracted by certain apparent and easily assimilable aspects of Indian religious and philosophical thought. References to such matters in both the prose and poetry of the period most often consist of catchwords or rather vague (at times purposefully vague) allusions to this or that facet of Hinduism or Buddhism more or less familiar in the West. One of the most prominent figures in this connection is Konstantin Bal'mont (1867-1942) who, however, unlike the great majority of his fellow poets in and outside of Russia had himself studied Sanskrit and visited India (1912). Thus, of the two epigraphs to a group of his poems, *Indijskie travy* (1899), one is the familiar *Tat tvam asi* (*To est' ty*), the *mahāvākya* or "great proposition" of the Upaniṣads, a phrase that one encounters quite frequently in philosophically or mystically minded authors.[3] The other epigraph, *Poznavshij sushchnost' stal vyshe pechali*, is attributed to "Shri-Shankara-Acharija" (i.e., *Śaṅkara*), the founder of the classical Vedānta system of philosophy who died about 820 A.D. Bal'mont gives an Indian and Hindu coloration to the poems *Majja* (*māyā*), *Indijskij motiv*, and *Indijskij mudrets* by introducing a scattering of suggestive words (*tigry*, *champak*, *iogi*, *mantra*, *Brama*, *lotos*, *slon*)[4] and he includes, in *Majja*, two verses that reflect a Vedānta viewpoint:

> For the ignorant, life is delusion; for the yogi
> It is illusion, a soulless ocean of silence!

The "ring-form" (*kol'tso*) of *Majja* is also significant.

Given Bal'mont's exotic tastes and his wide range of esoteric themes, it is not surprising that he should also have written a poem entitled *Yoni-Lingam* (in the collection *Prazdnik serdtsa*, 1904). The verses here are addressed to the "tensely powerful Lingam" (the Hindu phallic symbol) and the "receptively moist Yoni" (the representation of the female genitals). The poem is eclectic, with allusions to Aphrodite, Adonis, Isis, Ishtar, Pan, and Melitta but with a significant ending—a reference to the androgynous (*androginnyj*) Śiva, "he who united Yoni and Lingam".

Among Bal'mont's numerous translations from the poetry of various languages there are four short poems *iz indijskoj poèzii* (of the eighteenth century), published in *Severnye zapiski* in 1915 (No. 1, pp. 91-92) and included with his complete poems. The first three are distichs by Mir Taqi, Shah Selim, and Mian Jangu, while the fourth is a version of a ghazal by Mir Soz. Bal'mont's version of Mir Taqi's lines runs:

> Mysl' prinikaet do chernykh volos tvoikh,—na litse
> /moem slezy toski,
> I divljusja, no nochi mne grezjatsja, bryzzhet dozhd',
> /i gorjat svetljaki.

A somewhat closer translation, but one which also retains the rhyme, is that of Ralph Russell and Khurshidul Islam:

> Your long black tresses come to mind and glistening
> /teardrops dim my sight.
> And all is dark; the rains have come; the fireflies
> /glimmer in the night.[5]

Mir Taqi Mir (1722-1810) was, incidentally, one of the greatest of the Mughal Urdu poets.[6]

Bal'mont also published a translation of the *Buddhacarita*, a metrical life of the Buddha by Aśvaghoṣa, the most important of the Buddhist writers of Sanskrit (first century A.D.). This is the *Zhizn' Buddy* (Moscow, 1913) which includes an introduction by the distinguished French Sanskrit scholar, Sylvain Lévi. In 1914 and 1915 brief selections of *aforizmy* derived from Bhartṛhari were published in *Severnye zapiski* (No. 10-11, 1914, pp. 238-241; No. 1, 1915, pp. 85-90). Bal'mont's interest in Indian patterns of thought carried over into his well-known study, *Poèzija kak volshebstvo* ("Poetry as Magic", 1915). Here he quotes (in Russian) the Vedas and makes some remarks reminiscent of Lomonosov's eighteenth-century poetics, claiming that the vowel-sounds have connotations of their own: this is why, he writes, the names of Hindu women contain so many a-sounds, why the world-snake in Hindu mythology is Ananta, etc.

But probably Bal'mont's most familiar translation is his version or adaptation of Kālidāsa's play *Śakuntalā*, which was chosen by Aleksandr Tairov for the opening-night presentation at the *Kamernyj Teatr* in 1914.[7] Bal'mont used a French translation of the Sanskrit classic as the basis of his adaptation which was published in Moscow in 1915. In the following year the *Śakuntalā*, together with two other plays by Kālidāsa, all translated from the French, appeared in an edition with an introductory article by the Sanskrit scholar, S. Ol'denburg.

An almost exact contemporary of Bal'mont was Dmitrij Merezhkovskij (1865-1941). A man of encyclopedic knowledge and a prolific writer, his name is always mentioned in connection with the Russian decadence and Russian symbolism, since his 1893 essay, "On the Causes of Decadence and on the New Tendencies in Modern Russian Literature", serves as a kind of manifesto and *confession de foi* of the modernists. Merezhkovskij's oft commented-on preoccupation with death and his marked penchant for systems of mysticism no doubt attracted him to certain aspects of Hindu and especially Buddhist religious thought. One of his most familiar poems in this latter connection is *Nirvana* (1896), a short poem which ends "What joy not to think,/What pleasure not to desire!". His *Budda* (1886) is longer and contains some good lines, such as

Death will take all that is dear.
He who loved thee will fall out of love.
Joy flashes by like a spectre.
There's no salvation! Glory, fortune,
Love and beauty—all will fade away
Like the colors of the bright rainbow
In foul weather.

But the poem as a whole smacks more of the Christian *Dies irae, dies illae* theme than of Buddhism. *Sak'ja Muni* (1885), with its reference to a giant Buddha with a "porphyry crown" containing a huge diamond near the banks of the Ganges, is quite weak. *Vostochnyj mif* (1888), also about the Buddha and a variation of the Barlaam and Josaphat story referred to in Chapter I, is a fairly good narrative poem, despite Merezhkovskij's lines about a "row of huge porphyry columns with caryatids of carved elephants".

Orvasi is a short dramatic poem, an adaptation of a passage in Kālidāsa's play, *Vikramorvaśīya* ("Valor-won Urvashī"), based on the story of King Pururavas and the nymph Urvaśī in the *Śatapatha Brāhmaṇa*. Merezhkovskij's poem, which first appeared in *Severnyj vestnik* (No. 8, 1886), is a pleasing work, effectively decked out with many suggestive words and phrases (*mimozy, banany, peri, slon, kokosovaja roshcha, pavlin, giatsinty, bambukovaja chashcha, lebed', lotos, etc.*) and retaining significant details—e.g., *luna v korone Sivy* (i.e., Śiva as *candramukuṭa*). *Arivanza*—or *Iz Arivanzy* (1886)—is a short poem based, as the title indicates, on a passage in the *Harivaṃśa* ("the family of Kṛṣṇa"), the supplement to the *Mahābhārata*, while *Zhertva* (1886) is a retelling of the story of Uśīnara in the *Mahābhārata* who was severely tested by the god Indra.

Valerij Brjusov (1873-1924), another of the early Russian symbolist poets, had a rather exotic taste and his verse-forms and subject-matter cover a surprisingly wide range. One of his early poems, *Na zhurchashchej Godaveri* (1894) refers to the practice of Indian women divining the future by placing flowers on banana leaves and setting these afloat on the Godāvarī: the upsetting of the leaves predicts unhappiness. Several deities are addressed in the poem: *boginja Schast'ja* (i.e., Lakṣmī or Śrī), Kāma (the god of love), and Kālī (the consort of Śiva), amongst others. Another group of five poems, entitled by Brjusov simply *Podrazhanie stikham Amaru*, was written in 1913. The "Amaru" referred to is the *Amaruśataka*, a collection (as noted in the preceding chapter) of amatory verse by poets of the seventh and eighth centuries. I quote in translation the first of Brjusov's poems which is clearly in the Amaru style:

> Rain! I bless thee!
> Thou didst soak her clothes:
> How clearly beneath the damp fabric
> The body of my beloved was outlined!
> Thou wert as one full naked,
> And thy breasts shivered!
> But who warmed them with a kiss
> As the rainbow sparkled?

Podrazhanie Rabindranatu Tagoru (1913) is an adaptation, in three stanzas, of a four-stanza poem by Rabindranath Tagore, who seems to have been as popular in Russia as in England and America.[8] Brjusov's first stanza reads:

> When I bring you toys, my children,
> I see clearly why the clouds gleam like pearls,
> And why the south wind clings so caressingly to flowers,
> When I bring you toys, my children.

This is quite close to Tagore's own English prose translation of the original Bengali poem (which begins *Ranin khelna dile o rana hate*), of which the first stanza is: "When I bring you coloured toys, my child, I understand why there is such a play of colours on clouds, on water, and why flowers are painted in tints—when I give coloured toys to you, my child".[9]

Of the three major poets in the younger—or second—generation of Russian symbolists (the "realist" symbolists), Aleksandr Blok (1880-1921) is the most renowned. But there is scarcely a mention of India in either his prose or poetry. However, in his diary (for 9 January, 1918) he does make the following unusual allusion: "Truth is accessible only to fools. Kālidāsa, in order to become himself, had, being a fool, to learn (acc. to the legend) to become wise. This, I think, is a corrupted legend (some kind of late and bookish one)". This is a reference to one of several legends associated with the name of Kālidāsa, the Sanskrit playwright and poet. He was, according to this legend, born a brāhmaṇa but orphaned at an early age, reared by an ox-driver, and grew up uneducated. A rejected suitor of a princess of Banaras, in order to play a cruel joke on the princess, brought in the handsome young man, dressed him in the garments of a scholar, admonished him to remain silent, and introduced him to the princess. She fell in love with him but he remained silent, as instructed. Seeing on one occasion the image of a bull, he blurted out some rustic language. The princess, shocked, told him to pray to the goddess Kālī. This he did, and knowledge and the gift of poetry descended upon him miraculously. In gratitude, he took the name Kālidāsa ("servant of Kāli").[10]

Andrej Belyj (his real name was Boris Bugaev, 1880-1934), who speaks in almost ecstatic terms of the impression that a reading of the Upaniṣads made on him as an adolescent and of how his aspirations in later years were influenced by the Vedas, has a number of allusions to India in both his prose and poetry.[11] In *Na rubezhe dvukh stoletij* (1929) he also mentions his interests in Buddhism and Schopenhauer.[12] In his long poem *Pervoe svidanie* (1921), for example, Belyj refers to the Upaniṣads and to Ānanda, a disciple of Buddha, and uses the term *anupadaka*: he means, presumably, *anupapādaka* ("having no material parents", the name of a class of Buddhas). Belyj also refers here to "Darmotarra" (i.e., Dharmottara), a famous Buddhist teacher and disciple of Dharmakīrti in the Dignāga school. Belyj himself had read the *Nyāyabindu*, a textbook on logic by Dharmakīrti, in Shcherbatskoj's Russian translation (1904) and in his novel, *Peterburg*, he mentions that Nikolaj Apollonovich, a devotee of Buddhism, has also read this work.

In that odd little book, *Glossalogija* (1922), which Mochulsky refers to as a work of "anthroposophical linguistics", Belyj (for a time a student of Rudolf Steiner and his Anthroposophy) demonstrates an elementary acquaintance with Indo-European philology and Sanskrit. He mentions F. Max Müller and seems to have looked over a Sanskrit grammar. Discussing the significance of the Cyrillic letter "d", he writes: "The banyan tree of the Buddha (a network of nerves [i.e., the *arbor vitae cerebelli*]), having grown its crown (our brain), produces ripe fruit: it blooms in the form of a sound and issues from the brain as the growth of a sound: we see ornaments".

Then there is the highly syncretic and esoteric symbolism in the article "Émblematika smysla" (1909) and in *Kotik Letaev* (1918), especially that of the triad/trinity/triangle (including the Buddhist triad "Ātma-Buddhi-Manas"), drawn from various sources but chiefly from the writings of Helen Blavatsky (whose influence on Yeats is also well known). Thus in "Émblematika smysla" Belyj writes: "The teaching concerning the new man and the coming fate of Aryan culture is a summons to the creation of the personality and a reflection of obsolete ethical forms. All of this we may encounter in those philosophical and religious currents of India which are as old as the world itself".[13]

A great number of images and allusions in the poetry of Vjacheslav Ivanov (1866-1949) are drawn from classical mythology (Ivanov was a classical scholar) and the Bible; but there is also frequent mention of India or aspects of India. We find, for instance, in Ivanov's second volume of verse, *Prozrachnost'* (1904), a three-part poem entitled *Sloki* (i.e., ślokas).[14] Ivanov has imitated here the *triṣṭubh* śloka (or stanzaic form), consisting of four "feet" (or quarters)—we would call them lines—of eleven syllables each (unrhymed). The first part of the poem has three ślokas, the second two, and the third only one. I quote here in translation the first śloka of the first part:

> Who will say: "Here is fire" of cold ashes
> Or of damp wood stacked in storage?
> Fire burns; and, moving, force moves;
> And the will wills; and where will is, action is.

There are no references, here or elsewhere in the poem, to anything specifically Indian; but the overall tone of the poem is Upaniṣadic and of course the sequence of ślokas (3 plus 2 plus 1) is symbolic. One can see, behind certain capitalized Russian words, the Sanskrit equivalents: *Pokoj* (*prasāda*, *śāntatva*), *Alchba* (*vana*), *Dejan'e* (*karma*), etc.

Several other examples of Indian allusions may be found in the major collection entitled *Cor Ardens* (1912). *Uzly zmei*, for instance, which begins with a reference to Ivanov's earlier *Veneris figurae*,[15] seems to suggest that the author had in mind the erotic sculpture on a Hindu temple. Here in translation are the second and third stanzas:

Three hundred thirty-three temptations, three-three-three/ways to strike—
(For the weak—perdition) for those whose bright hearts/are diamond-like,
For those,—deeds of ardent pain. Yogis and rishis of the Ganges
Rolled a long scroll out for them—from the beginning to /the ending.
In lust's menacing rhythm, to the phial of knowledge's /conflagration,
Approach, Brahman, with your lips which are already scorched /and hot,
So that from the wheels of holy calms, cries of last incantations
Could together bring in one hold all the burning bridles' knots.[16]

In the sonnet-sequence *Zolotye zavesy* there is an incongruous mixture of allusions—to St. Sebastian, Greek mythology, Paolo and Francesca, the Egyptian god Ra, etc. And in Sonnet XI there is the line

> As in a storm the Gandharvas' musical rumble

(the Gandharvas are the singers and musicians of the gods in Hindu mythology); and in Sonnet XII the quatrain:

> Stronghold of secrets and hermitage of Indian
> Charms, Tibet nurtured the clan of thy forebears,
> And on the submissive brow was impressed
> The humbly-wise light of Buddhist suns.

It might be noted here, by the way, that Ivanov (like some of the other symbolists) makes rather extensive use in his verse of compound adjectives, reminding us of a similar usage in certain works of early Muscovite literature[17] but even more of the extreme development of compounding in Sanskrit. This development in turn produced an elaborate Sanskrit terminology for various types of compounds which modern linguists employ. For example, the Russian compound *smirennomudryj* ("humble and wise") in the above stanza is a dvandva (copulative or coordinate) compound, like the Sanskrit *aruṇababhru* ("red and brown"), whereas an adjective like *dlinnovolosyj* (like the Sanskrit *dīrghakeśa*) is a bahuvrīhi compound.

Among Ivanov's *gazely* (ghazals) *o roze* there is one (IV) with a reference to the "rose of Kashmir"; and in *Antologija rozy*, consisting of elegiac distichs, there is one entitled *Lotos*:

Mudrost'! Na utrennem Gange Ty Lotosom vodnym prisnilas':

Rozoj zemnoj rastsvela v arimafejskoj teni.

The association here of the Ganges and Arimathea (and the legend of Joseph of Arimathea) is unusual but typical of Ivanov's highly syncretic imagery.

In the collection *Svet vechernij* (Oxford University Press, 1962) Ivanov has a poem, *Golub' i chasha*, with the words "...nebosvod/ Perelivaetsja Golkondoju zhemchuzhin". Golconda, where there is now a fortress and ruins, is just west of Hyderabad city and was once famous as a cutting-place and market for diamonds from neighboring mines (the Koh-i-Nur diamond was found nearby in 1623). Though to speak of a "Golconda of pearls" is, strictly, incorrect, Ivanov no doubt is using *Golkonda* in the sense of a "treasure-house". (In Chapter II we mentioned Ivanov's poem *Kitovras* in connection with the *Povest' o Solomone i Kitovrase*.)

In a poem dedicated to Vjacheslav Ivanov, "Gnostic Hymn to the Virgin Mary" (1907), Maksimilian Voloshin (1877-1932), another but less familiar symbolist poet, refers to *māyā* and *parabrahman* (the Supreme Spirit or Brahman). Voloshin is, incidentally, the only Russian poet here noted to employ (line 5) a Sanskrit technical term in Latin rather than in Cyrillic transliteration: *Mula-Pracriti* (i.e., *mūla-prakṛti*), the original, undifferentiated source or "root" (*mūla*) of matter, the first emanation of Parabrahman.

Innokentij Annenskij (1856-1909), a Greek scholar, was a contemporary of the symbolists who wrote verse that is highly elliptical and, on occasion, cryptic rather than symbolist. Among Annenskij's translations there are several versions of Leconte de Lisle and, among these, there are two poems with allusions to India. In *Majja* (1904), which begins

O Maya, O stream of elusive chimaeras,
From the heart thou bringest a fountain of living wonders!
There the moment of pleasure, the gall of unseen tears,
The dark world of the soul, the bright lustre of the sky,

we have an adaptation of the French poet's *La Maya* (in *Poèmes tragiques*), beginning

Maya! Maya! torrent des mobiles chimères,
Tu fais jaillir du coeur de l'homme universel
Les brèves voluptés, et les haines amères,
Le monde obscur des sens et la splendeur du ciel.

The other poem, *Negibnushchij aromat* (1904), a version of *Le parfum impérissable* (also in *Poèmes tragiques*), has only a reference to Lahore to relate the contents of the poem to India.

2

Associated with Acmeism, one of the more significant post-symbolist movements, were several outstanding Russian poets, including Nikolaj Gumilev (1886-1921). Gumilev, whose ethnographical interests took him on different occasions to Abyssinia and Somaliland, wrote romantic verse that is exceptionally rich in references to exotic lands and peoples, including India.[18] One of his finest similes occurs in *Pjatistopnye jamby*, first written in 1912 but later revised in part, where the relationship between Nala and Damayantī (in a famous episode of the *Mahābhārata*) is used very effectively:

I have lost thee as once
The frenzied Nala his Damayanti lost.[19]

Severnyj radzha (1910) is a three-part poem dedicated to "Valentin Krivich" (pseudonym of Innokentij Annenskij's son) with a striking and unusual combination of lexical elements associated with India (*radzha*, *lotos*, *slony*, *barsy*) and others associated with Russia and the North (*led*, *sneg*, *eli*, *v'jugi*). In the familiar and oft-anthologized *Zabludivshijsja tramvaj* (1921) the phrase *V Indiju Dukha* occurs; here *Indiju* might be glossed by a phrase such as *basnoslovnuju zemlju.* In *Goncharova i Larionov*, published posthumously and sub-titled *pantum*, Gumilev weaves the stanzas in the pantum-manner (the second and fourth lines of each stanza become the first and third lines of the next), e.g.,

V sebe otkryla Goncharova
Pavlin'ikh krasok bred i pen'e,
U Larionova surovo
Zheleznogo ognja kruzhen'e.

Pavlin'ikh krasok bred i pen'e
Ot Indii do Vizantii,
Zheleznogo ognja kruzhen'e—
Voj pokorjaemoj stikhii.

Ot Indii do Vizantii
Kto dremlet, esli ne Rossija?
Voj pokorjaemoj stikhii—
Ne obnovlennaja l' stikhija?

Though the pantum (or pantun) is actually a Malayan verse-form, it probably originated in jingling variations on the ślokas of the *Rāmāyaṇa* and *Mahābhārata*. The form was introduced into Europe by the French orientalist Ernest Fouinet and later employed by the French symbolist poets. Natal'ja Goncharova and Mikhail Larionov were two of the most gifted pre-revolutionary Russian modernist painters.

Anna Akhmatova (1889-1966), another important figure in the Acmeist group, although we find little of India in her own poetry (aside from rare phrases like *polja Kashmira* in *Luna v zenite*), also did some translations (on the basis of intermediate prose renditions) of Indian poetry. She was, for instance, one of the translators, along with Pasternak, of poems by Rabindranath Tagore published in *Vostochnyj al'manakh* (Moscow, 1957). I quote here in translation the opening lines of her free version of *Afrika*, a poem written by Tagore in 1942:

In that distant and most troubled age
When the creator, vexed with his creations,
Destroyed all that he himself had made...
On that day when, from his wrath,
The earth in panic began to shake,
In a flash the Red Sea's hands, O Africa,
Tore thee away from the land,
Severing thee from mother East,
And set thee down midst forested mountains,
There, where the light hardly ever glimmers,
And left thee to the whim of fate.[20]

Tagore's Bengali poem first appeared in the collection *Patraput* and was translated into English by the poet himself. For the sake of comparison, I give the opening of this translation:

In that early dusk of a distracted age,
when God in scorn of his workmanship
violently shook his head at his primitive efforts,
an impatient wave snatched you away, Africa,
from the bosom of the East,
and kept you brooding in a dense enclosure of niggardly
night...[21]

Akhmatova is also among the contributing translators in *Poèty Indii* (Tashkent, 1958) and *Bengal'skaja poèzija* (Moscow-Leningrad, 1959). *Golosa poètov* (Moscow, 1965) contains Akhmatova's versions of poems by Tagore and Sumitrānandan Pant. Still other versions of Pant by Akhmatova appeared in *Izbrannye stikhi* (Moscow, 1959).

Another Acmeist—and one of the greatest Russian poets—was Osip Mandel'shtam (1891-1938). His deep and consuming passion for Hellenism and the Christian tradition left little room for the Orient, including India.[22] Thrice, however, he makes use of the adjective *buddijskij* in his verse. The striking phrase *buddijskaja Moskva* occurs, for example, in the following context:

In the year nineteen-thirty-one
I returned—no, read: by force
Was I returned to Buddhist Moscow.[23]

The phrase seems more than a mere equivalent of "Asiatic Moscow". Nadezhda Mandel 'shtam in her memoirs quotes the second and third lines, explaining that her husband regarded certain mechanical forms of motion and activity as essentially immobility and "Buddhism".[24] Some aspects of all religious systems—including Christianity—may be viewed and discussed in pejorative terms; and Buddhism has often been treated this way in the West, especially in literary metaphor. Aside from the critical (and often humorous) definitions in Soviet "reference" works,[25] we find this derogatory view of both Buddhism and Hinduism in, for example, Herzen, and we know that Mandel'shtam was markedly influenced by Herzen when he was young.[26]

But Mandel'shtam also refers in another poem (*Polnoch' v Moskve*[27]) to the "sumptuously Buddhist summer" (*roskoshno buddijskoe leto*), where the allusion is not derogatory and the meaning presumably is something like "exotic" or "eastern". In still another poem the poet has the following lines:

> If you want to live, then look with a smile
> On milk that's Buddhist blue...[28]

Here *buddijskaja sineva* refers to that particular effect of blue seen on the surface of skim milk and seems to suggest the Chinese term *ying ch'ing* ("shadow-blue") used of pottery on which a blue tinge appears in deep translucent glaze.

Sergej Gorodetskij (b. 1884), best known for his collection of verse entitled *Jar'* (1907), was later briefly associated with the Acmeists but became a Communist after 1917. His reaction to Gumilev's death before a firing squad in 1921 and his own servile attitude to the Party paralleled his decline as a poet. He has a poem entitled *Indija* (1922) in the collection *Alaja neft'* which, though in it he happily avoids references to the Ganges and dancing-girls, is perhaps the worst poem on India of those noted in this book. I quote the third stanza:

> In cold, in blood, we in the far white North
> Have become free; and to you, terrorized by the lash,
> To you, patiently suffering shameful torment,
> To you we extend the youthful hand of friendship.[29]

The poets affiliated with another important post-symbolist movement, Russian Futurism, were not in general attracted by Oriental—and specifically Indian—imagery and themes. This is particularly true of Vladimir Majakovskij. But the prose and poetry of Velimir Khlebnikov (1885-1922) contain numerous references to Indian subject-matter.[30] In *Khadzhi Tarkhan* (1913), for example, occur the lines:

> And the soul of India prayed
> To the lowly blade of grass,

where the *bylinka* is very likely an allusion to the sacred Hindu grass or *kuśa*. In the same poem Khlebnikov refers to Astrakhan' as a "window", reminding us of Pushkin on Peter the Great:

> Through the Russians, to India,
> To the window, the merchant ships
> Brought arms and grain.[31]

Edinaja kniga (1920) begins "Ja videl, chto chernye Vedy,...". The reference to "black Vedas" is not at all arbitrary and illustrates the degree of Khlebnikov's knowledge at least concerning the Vedic texts. The recensions of the *Yajurveda* (the "sacrificial Veda", containing sacrificial formulas or mantras) exist in two forms, one of which (the *Taittirīyasaṃhitā*) is known as the "Black Veda" (*kṛṣṇayajurveda*). *Edinaja kniga* also contains the lines,

> And the Ganges, where the dark folk
> Are the trees of the mind.[32]

In *Ladomir* (1920), a complex philosophical poem, Khlebnikov, who loved to play with sounds and syllables, has these lines:

> Where the Volga says "I",
> The Yangtze Kiang mutters "love",
> And the Mississippi says "the",
> The old Danube mutters "whole",
> And the Ganges says "world".

And further on in the same poem there is mention of *Tièn* (usually transliterated *tjan'* in Russian)—i.e., the Chinese *t'ien* (sky, heaven)—conversing with Indra.

India is referred to briefly in the long and complex work in prose and verse, *Deti vydry* (1913); this is based on a cosmological myth of the Mongolian Orochi people (the title, "Children of the Otter", is an allusion to the otter as an Orochi totem). In this poem Khlebnikov associates—attempts, in fact, a synthesis of—eastern and western myths.[33] In *Ispaganskij verbljud* (1921) the Ganges and the Volga are associated symbolically in a manner that reminds one of baroque usage or eighteenth-century odes ("Ot Volgi do Ganga").

Finally, in the story *Esir* (written in 1916) there are many allusions to India: *Aurengzeb*, *Vishnu*, *Nanak*, *Govinda*, *Brakhma*, *Majja*, *Shvetambar* (i.e., the *śvetāmbara* sect of Jainism), etc. An Indian, Krishnamūrti, appears, repeating the sacred syllable *Aum*, and with the *lebed' vremeni* or *Kala-Gamza* (i.e., *kalahaṃsa*) above his head. In the short prose piece *Son* (1916) one is surprised to encounter a technical term of Hindu philosophy, *agankara* (i.e., *ahaṃkāra*, self-consciousness or the activity of making the consciousness an object). And again the Volga and the Ganges are brought together: "The water of the Ganges flows into the dark waters of the Volga—the Northern Bride!"

Khlebnikov, although he never visited India (he was, however, in Persia in 1921), picked up, as we see, a good deal of information on Hinduism and Buddhism. He was particularly attracted to the latter, especially its teachings on brotherhood and equality and on the harmony between the lives of men and animals. A fragment of a symbolist sketch that Khlebnikov wrote in 1915 opens with the words: "I went to Ashoka and asked him to lend me some thoughts on equality and fraternity".[34]

Boris Pasternak (1890-1960), who translated some of Tagore's verse,[35] introduces an occasional Indian image in his own poetry —e.g., the inevitable Ganges, as in *Toska* (1922), where there is also a reference to Kipling, and in the third poem (beginning "Mchalis' zvezdy") in *Variatsii* (1918). Bodo Zelinsky has some interesting comments on the latter poem with its oriental allusions, and he compares it rather extensively with other poems by Pushkin, Lermontov, and Solov'ev.[36] Pasternak also has a version of Shelley's *The Indian Serenade* (1822); but he omits in his translation Shelley's only specific Indian allusion (to the champac tree).[37]

3

Among the older generation of Soviet Russian poets, Nikolaj Tikhonov (b. 1896), who visited the Near and Far East as well as India, has by far the greatest number of references to India in his verse. But his Indian poems are rather banal, filled with stale clichés, mawkish, or crudely political. In romantic *Indija* (one of his early poems, 1913-1920), which begins "Strana jogi, radzhi i fakira/ Zemlja Tanzhora, Vishnu, Ganga, Ved",[38] there is mention of Indian rivers, cities, and monuments as well as the familiar bronze figurines of Kāli, the "mournful ghats", and the Tāj Mahal which blinds the eye with its "pearly whiteness". In the more politically oriented *Indijskij son* (in *Poiski geroja*, 1923-1929) the "dream" recalls the incident of 13 April 1920 in Amritsar when troops under British General Dyer (he was later censured and retired from the service) dispersed a large but prohibited meeting in the Jalliānwālā Bāgh by firing without warning into the crowd: 379 persons were killed and 1200 wounded.[39] Making his reappearance in this poem is an Indian youth, Sami, the hero of an earlier ballad of the same name published in 1920.[40] In *Sami* the young man of Amritsar is "reborn" after praying to "Lenni" (Lenin). Although Grinberg calls *Sami* "one of the most remarkable achievements of Soviet poetry" and although it is sometimes called Kiplingesque,[41] it is actually more akin to something Evtushenko might have written. Incidentally, S. Rozanov based an Indian episode in his play *Bud' gotov*! (Moscow, 1925) on Tikhonov's *Sami*. The play ran in the Moscow Theatre for Children from 1924 to 1926.[42]

In the brief *Ind* Tikhonov refers to the "mighty Indus"; *Ind*, *Dva bljudtsa iz Dakki*, *Zebu*, *Kholmy za Raval'pindi*, and *Chili* (all in the collection *Dva potoka*, 1951) recall Tikhonov's visit to Pakistan in 1949. *Chili* (i.e., chils—Sanskrit *cīlla*, kite), subtitled *Korshuny*, with its pictures of kites or chils swarming over the port of Karachi and of starving and naked Pakistanis, is an anti-colonialist poem.

Tikhonov also "translated" (via a prepared prose version in Russian) several of the Urdu poems of Faiz (Ahmad Faiz), a radical leftist poet living in exile in Pakistan. He also wrote forewords to collections of modern Indian "proletarian" tales in translation (*Indijskie rasskazy*, 1953; *Indijskie i pakistanskie rasskazy*, 1954). And Tikhonov himself dealt with Indian themes in his prose. A representative example is the tale *Seryj Khanuman* (1968).[43] The story concerns two Swiss journalists in India, more particularly one of them, who has written modernist fiction that reflects his uninvolved relationship with reality. Through a series of incidents and contact with "real" Indians—especially Ram Das who spouts "progressive" jargon—he begins to see the light and we can imagine him on the way towards socialist realism.

Pavel Antokol'skij in his essay on Tikhonov writes the following concerning *Sami*:

> When, at the beginning of the twenties, Tikhonov's poem about the young Indian, Sami, appeared, the author did not

realize that his short poem would, like a letter sealed in a bottle, float not only into the Mediterranean and Red seas, not only into the Indian Ocean, but that it would float into the *sea of time* and would, in the forties, reach the banks of the Ganges at the same time that the author himself turned up there as one of the first Soviet writers to visit India.[44]

Nikolaj Zabolotskij (1903-1958), one of the more interesting of the Soviet poets, found it increasingly difficult to adapt to Soviet realities and was arrested and exiled for a number of years during the Stalinist purges. He was very much interested in Georgian poetry, which he translated extensively, and numerous Georgian and Caucasian themes are found in his own verse. Though Zabolotskij has no poems concerned specifically with India, his "Mongolian" poems are worth mentioning here. One of these is *Snezhnyj chelovek* (1957), the only poem I know of—in Russian or any other literature—which employs the image of the "Abominable Snowman" or yeti of the Himalayas:

> They say that somewhere in the Himalayas,
> Above the temples and the monasteries,
> He lives, a stranger to the light,
> Savage offspring of the beasts.[45]

The legendary creature is later referred to as *Gimalajskij ètot troglodit*. In his long poem, *Rubruk v Mongolii*,[46] Zabolotskij has the Tibetans repeating the words *Om mani padme kum*!, the sacred Buddhist formula addressed in Tibet only to the patron "saint" of Lhasa, Shenrezig.

But in the great gray mass of officially recognized Soviet poetry in that long, dreary period that sets in after the penultimate reverberations of symbolism and its successor movements had faded away; and, especially, after the dread effects of "socialist realism" became apparent, though we continue to find allusions to India, these are apt to be either crude, commonplace, or maudlin. Indeed, it would be both painful and boring to catalog many examples, but I shall cite a few. Eduard Dzjubin (Bagritskij, 1897-1934), better known for his *Duma pro Opanasa*, has, for instance, in the poem *Vostok i zapad* (1926), translated (together with N. Dement'-ev) from the Turkish of Nazim Hikmet (1902-1963), the following lines concerning British officers in India:

They dip their black toes into the Ganges
Where float the white-toothed bodies of Indians.

Igor' Lotarev (Igor'-Severjanin, 1887-1941) has an unusual reference to Kipling as one familiar with the exotic flora—as well as the scripts—of India in his poem, *I bylo stranno ee pis'mo* (1929): the poet has received an almost illegible letter, the ductus of which only a Kipling could follow. In his long *Majakovskij nachinaetsja* (1940) Nikolaj Aseev (1889-1963), whose verses, as Anna Akhmatova once remarked, are not "stikhi, a rifmovannoe zajavlenie v Mossovet", recalls with contempt the decadent early nineteen-hundreds in Russia and the outlandish things one could see, such as

In the shop windows
Books by Indian scholars.

In the more recent past, Anatolij Sofronov (b. 1911) has in the collection *Poèma proshchanij* (1968-1970) one longish poem, *Gimalai*, in which he recalls a flight to India over the Himalayas:

I flew to Calcutta
        and Bombay,
And admired the Ganges;
And a good friend
        for friends
In India I remained.
How's my friend Abbas?
        How's friend Anand?
How's Romesh Chandra getting on?
Friendship, you know, is like a talent:
Once formed,
        it lasts forever.[47]

And among the verse published in the sixties by the Leningrad poet, Viktor Sosnora (b. 1936), there is *Rozy*, with the lines:

The roses
In every milligram of ink
That Pushkin, Shelley, Tagore used.

4

In the preceding chapter we mentioned some of Lev Tolstoj's minor works having to do with Indian sources as well as Konstantin Leont'ev's and de Vogüé's comments on Tolstoj himself. But Tolstoj's real interest in India began in 1908 with his epistolary article, *Pis'mo k indusu*, addressed to Tāraknāth Dās who advocated violent resistance to British rule in India.[48] In his article Tolstoj advocates non-resistance and says that if multitudes in India have been enslaved by the violence of a few—the British, it is because the Indians themselves have lived by and perpetuated violence. The letter was widely publicized and it caught the attention of Gāndhī who was then in South Africa. Gāndhī wrote Tolstoj and a correspondence ensued. The future Indian leader sent Tolstoj a copy of his book, *Indian Home Rule*, and referred to Tolstoj as the "Russian titan".[49] But more detailed accounts are readily available in studies by Alexandre Kaplan, K. Nag and Martin Green.[50]

Ivan Bunin (1870-1953), the first Russian writer to win a Nobel Prize in literature (1933), wrote both prose and poetry. Before he left Russia in 1918, he traveled widely in Europe and the Orient and visited Ceylon (now Sri Lanka) in 1911 where he was impressed, as most tourists are, by the remains of the ancient capital, Anuradhapura. Bunin recalls some of his impressions in *Gorod tsarja tsarej* (1925). Although Bunin seems to have believed that the name Anuradhapura means the "city of the king of kings" (it actually means the "city of the constellation Anurādhā", having been so named by King Pandukabhaya in the fourth century B.C.), he provides an interesting account of the island. He mentions, for example, Mahinda (the Buddhist apostle to Ceylon), King Tissa, the Bo-tree, the Thuparama dagobas, the Moonstones, etc. But Bunin seems to have been impressed even more by Buddhism itself rather than simply by its monuments, and we can see some of the effects of his newly-gained knowledge in the philosophical meditation entitled *Noch'* (1925).[51] Some of his Ceylon impressions and memories are also found in his fiction: in, for example, *Brat'ja* (1914), the sad story of a Singhalese rickshaw boy.[52] Another very short incident, *Sto rupij*, written much later (1944), tells how the narrator, having admired a beautiful girl from his hotel window in Colombo, is later offered her for a hundred rupees.

Indian and Ceylonese allusions also occur in Bunin's verse. In

Sudra (1905) he uses the sudra (Skt. *śūdra*, the lowest of the four Hindu classes) theme to express his own sense of alienation and nostalgia for the past:

> The dead have left their clothes, and
> The poor sudra wears them. So to me
> Life leaves not joy and hope,
> But only sorrow over the past.

In the sonnet *Agni* (1906) the poet calls upon Agni, the god of fire and the intermediary between gods and men, to rescue him from darkness. In another poem, *Tsejlon* (1915), he sees Mt. Alagala rising on the horizon like a gray mastodon; and in another, longer *Tsejlon* (1916) Bunin recalls, in a kind of lyrical catalog, the flora and fauna of the island.

In an article entitled "Où l'orient et l'occident s'affrontent", Fernand Baldensperger writes the following:

> Pour la Russie enfin, qui semble lasse de ses deux siècles d'adaptation occidentale plus ou moins poussée, il n'y a guère d'hesitation sur le point de l'horizon d'où elle prétend voir venir la lumière, et Gorki, dans la collection *La Littérature mondiale*, a franchement invoqué la mentalité asiatique pour tutrice des temps nouveaux.[53]

Baldensperger's "La Littérature mondiale" refers to *Vsemirnaja literatura*, a publishing house founded by Maksim Gor'kij in 1918 and intended to provide "scientific" translations of certain works from various literatures of the world: some two hundred titles were published before "World Literature" became part of *Gosudarstvennoe izdatel'stvo* in 1924. But we know now that Gor'kij was hardly a spokesman for the slogan *Ex oriente lux*; even the Soviet sources clearly indicate that Gor'kij's views in this respect, although they changed from time to time, were essentially negative. Though Gor'kij did feel that every nation—including India and China—could contribute its share to world culture, his actual opinion is summed up in such statements as "the Oriental awaits eternal happiness and rest beyond the limits of the earth, in the region of the imagination" and "for the Orient, man has no intrinsic significance or value".[54] His views of Buddhism and Hinduism were particularly derogatory and he thought little of Gāndhī and Tagore.[55]

However, Gor'kij was sympathetic with the independence movement in India,[56] and his efforts on behalf of the *Vostochnaja kollegija* of "World Literature" were highly lauded by the Indologist, Academician S.F. Ol'denburg in his article, "O Gor'kom i ego rabote na nauku".[57] Ol'denburg also edited the journal *Vostok* published by the *Vostochnaja kollegija* and wrote the article "Indijskaja literatura" which was published in 1919 along with articles by other orientalists to acquaint the Russian reading public with the oriental literatures.[58]

The Eurasian movement, although it had nothing specifically to do with India and although some of its concepts had been voiced earlier, began formally about the year 1921 with the publication in Sofia of *Iskhod k Vostoku* ("Exodus to the East").[59] The authors were Prince Nikolaj Trubetskoj, P. Savitskij, P. Suvchinskij, and G. Florovskij. The gist of the essays in the volume was that the Russians are not simply Slavs but rather Eurasians; they belong to another, non-European cultural world having marked affiliations with the "Turanian" East and with Asia in general. In connection with this thesis, a number of evidential facts were adduced: like the steppe peoples, the Russians display *udal'* (boldness, daring); they have a penchant for ritual and contemplation and are ardorous seekers after the Truth. In addition—and with greater plausibility—Trubetskoj pointed to certain linguistic features common to both Slavic and Indo-Iranian within the Indo-European community of languages. Such similarities have frequently been noted, however, as we have seen; and I might add here some remarks on this score by Professor Burrow:

> Phonetically the most noteworthy common feature is the change of *s* to *sh* (>Slav. *ch*) after *k*, *r*, *i* and *u* in Indo-Iranian and Slavonic, and after *r* also in Lithuanian. This is unlikely to be a matter of chance, since the conditions under which the change takes place are so closely parallel. The conclusion which must be drawn is that at one time the two branches were in close geographical proximity, and that this innovation affecting IE *s* established itself over a limited area comprising Slavonic and Indo-Iranian, but excluding the rest of Indo-European... In the sphere of vocabulary Indo-Iranian shares with Baltic and

> Slavonic a considerable number of words which are not found in the other Indo-European languages...As can be seen, the parallelism between Indo-Iranian and Slavonic is not absolutely complete, because they differ in the treatment of that *s* which follows IE *k̂* (>Skt. *ś*, Slav. *s*). But in all other respects they agree, and the correspondence is too close for such changes to have taken place independently."[60]

A remarkable instance of such close correspondence between Russian and Sanskrit is provided by a passage in the *Kaṭha Upaniṣad* where a reference is made to the empirical or sensual self. The Sanskrit word used here is *madhvād*, "honey-eater", the equivalent of the Russian cledonism for "bear", *medved'*, which also means "honey-eater".[61]

A more thorough treatment of Trubetskoj's suggestions regarding Eurasian links was given by Roman Jakobson in his paper, "K kharakteristike evrazijskogo jazykovogo sojuza"[62]; here the status of the Eurasian linguistic group is supported by rigorous and wide-ranging linguistic analysis. It is, by the way, in another paper in a *Festschrift* in honor of Professor Jakobson that one of the contributors tells of finding traces of *vṛddhi* in Slavic.[63] *Vṛddhi*, very familiar to students of Sanskrit, is defined by the author (Zbigniew Golab) as a "type of secondary (denominative) adjective-generating derivation" (e.g., in Sanskrit, *mūla*, "root", and the *vṛddhi* form *maula*, "radical"): one of the author's examples is Slavic *gaj*<**gōjo*-<**gojo*-.

There is brief mention, here and there, of India and Buddhism in the writings of two Russians who, after leaving Russia, became closely associated in France with Existentialism—Lev Shestov (1866-1938) and Nikolaj Berdjaev (1874-1948). Berdjaev notes, for example, certain technical resemblances between the asceticism of Yoga and the mysticism of St. Simeon the New Theologian and he quotes Vivekānanda.[64]

Prince Petr Kropotkin (1842-1921), whose name is intimately associated with political anarchism, served in the army as a young man and took part in several geographical survey expeditions to the Far East, which participation earned him an entry in the *Bibliografija Indii*.[65] And in his *Ethics: Origin and Development* (1922) he contrasts the military predatoriness of the Christian West with what he takes to be the lofty altruism of ancient Hinduism by quoting four appropriate lines from the *Mahābhārata*.[66] Less notorious than Kropotkin but more familiar to students of Russian literature was the literary scholar, D.N. Ovsjaniko-Kulikovskij (1853-1920); the wide range of his knowledge and interests is clearly reflected in his collected writings, which include an extensive study of the origins and principles of the Vedas.[67]

There are some significant connections between India and the Roerich (Rerikh) family. Nikolaj Konstantinovich Rerikh (1874-1947), the son of a distinguished lawyer in a Russian family of Scandinavian origin (the name Rerikh is a variant of Rjurik), was born in St. Petersburg. He studied art at the Imperial Academy and in 1898 he was appointed to a professorship in the Imperial Archeological Institute. He traveled widely, especially in the governments of Pskov, Novgorod, and Tver', and gained his reputation as an artist by painting scenes of prehistoric Russian and Varangian life.[68] Later his name became even more familiar in connection with his stage designs for Russian ballets, most notably *Prince Igor'* and *Le Sacre du printemps.* He left Russia in 1917 and settled in the United States. In 1923 a Nicholas Roerich Museum was established in New York City and in the same year Rerikh went to India and, later, to Mongolia and Tibet.[69]

One of Nikolaj Rerikh's sons, Jurij (1902-1960), received his education in England, at Harvard University, and at the Sorbonne, and lived in India from 1923 until 1957, when he returned to the Soviet Union. Jurij N. Rerikh was a well known Soviet orientalist and Indologist, a specialist in Tibetan history and language.[70] Especially noteworthy is his article, "Indology in Russia", published in *The Journal of the Greater Indian Society* (No. 12, 1945).[71] Another son, Svjatoslav, a painter, remained in India. He has been honored by the Indian government and it is rather surprising to encounter his name as an Indian painter in a small book, *Jesus in Indian Paintings*, by R.W. Taylor. The author, however, is not too complimentary: "Svetoslav Roerich has several Christ-themed paintings. They all seem meaningful to him. One, 'Love Thy Neighbor', shows a blue-eyed blond. Roerich told me that it was a charismatic Christ and His most powerful, difficult, and needed teaching. I am inclined to think Roerich thinks and talks well beyond his ability to paint".[72]

5

The name of Rudyard Kipling has been mentioned more than once in this chapter and it may be recalled that Nadezhda Buchinskaja (1876-1952), the humorist and satirist, took her pseudonym, *Tèffi*, from Kipling (Taffy appears in the *Just So Stories* and in the poem "Merrow Down", 1902). It is especially interesting that the names and reputations of both Teffy and Kipling have been, so to speak, rehabilitated in Soviet Russia: there are now Soviet editions of the former's short stories, while the works of Kipling, who earlier was viewed chiefly as an apologist and mouthpiece of British colonial imperialism, are now discussed in Soviet comparative literature studies.[73]

Kipling himself read Pushkin and Lermontov (in French translation) when he attended the United Services College at Westward Ho! during the years 1878-1882.[74] Following the Russian Revolution, he developed a vehement hatred of Bolshevism and in a letter to Rider Haggard in 1925 he wrote: "A chap from Berlin has sent me the corpus of a book of letters from prisoners of the Bolshies, in those northern camps under the arctic circle...It's one of the most appalling glimpses into Hell that you ever did see...It is the horrible perversion and ingenuity of the torments, moral and physical, that makes one sick".[75] Kipling also has an ironic poem, "Russia to the Pacifists", about the overthrow of the tsarist regime and its possible consequences; I quote the last stanza:

> God rest you, merry gentlemen, and keep you in your mirth!
> Was ever kingdom turned so soon to ashes, blood, and earth?
> 'Twixt the summer and the snow—seeding-time and frost—
> Arms and victual, hope and counsel, name and country lost!
> Singing:—*Let down by the foot and the head—Shovel and smooth*
> *it all! So do we bury a Nation dead...* And who shall
> be next to fall, good sirs,
> With your good help to fall?

And some readers may also recall in *Kim* (1901) the disagreeable and angry Russian in the Hills near Simla who says such things as, "It is we who can deal with Orientals" and "We have nowhere left our mark yet. Nowhere!" This Russian insults and strikes a venerable lama and is physically attacked in return by Kim (Chapter XII).

Andrej Sinjavskij, in his brilliant essay on a bad poem by Evtushenko ("The Bratsk Hydroelectric Station"), finds appropriate occasion to recall Kipling's poem, "Evarra and His Gods", and he aptly quotes a number of lines.[76] Some years later, in his *Golos iz khora*, Sinjavskij, musing about the nature of the artistic image, recalls the story in the *Mahābhārata* of the beautiful maiden Tilottamā created by the master craftsman Viśvakarman who dances before Śiva (Sinjavskij mistakenly refers to Brahmā) and captivates the god: "And he, spellbound by her beauty and filled with the passion of love, in order continuously to admire her charms, created for himself another face looking southwards, a third gazing westwards, and a fourth turned to the north".[77]

Zinner, in his brief essay on Kipling in Russian literature, does not, of course, mention Sinjavskij; but, in addition to citing those Russian writers who admired Kipling (e.g., Olesha, Grin, Bagritskij, Babel') and some Russian writers who translated Kipling (e.g., S. Marshak and K. Simonov), he even mentions Soviet artists who were influenced by Kipling's sketches and illustrations, and he cites a study in this connection of the artist A. Pakhomov.[78] Zinner does mention, however, the fact that Tolstoj disliked Kipling (and lumped him with, of all people, the French decadents in *What Is Art*?). But Kipling admired Tolstoj and there is an echo of this admiration in "Tomlinson". In this poem, Tomlinson, an ordinary Englishman, appears before the tribunal of heaven to account for both his evil and good deeds, and Kipling has him allude, in defense of the latter, to Tolstoj. This poem by Kipling is cited by Lukács to illustrate the wide-ranging influence of Tolstoj.[79] Finally, the Formalist critic, Viktor Shklovskij, refers in a slightly puzzling passage in *A Sentimental Journey* (1923) to his article, "The Connection Between Plot Devices and General Stylistic Devices", as resembling Kipling's story, "How the Whale Got His Throat" (in *Just So Stories*); but presumably, as Richard Sheldon points out, the allusion to the suspenders in Kipling's story means that Shklovskij felt that he was able to survive adversities by always remembering his writing desk.[80]

6

In May of 1912 Sergej Djagilev's company presented the ballet *Le Dieu bleu* in Paris. This work, with an exotic Indian setting, was composed by Reynaldo Hahn and choreographed by Fokin.[81]

Although the ballet does not make it very clear, the "blue god" is Viṣṇu who is so colored in Hindu iconography. In 1923 the ballet *Ajanta Frescoes*, with music by Cherepnin and choreography by Clustine, premiered at Covent Garden in London. This was staged by the company of Anna Pavlova who had visited India in 1922 and had been particularly impressed by the Ajanta temple and caves. Also in 1923 Anna Pavlova met a young Indian dancer, Uday Shankar, then studying painting in London, and she asked him to do two ballets for her, *Hindu Wedding* and *Radha and Krishna* (both were later incorporated into *Oriental Impressions*). Pavlova encouraged Uday Shankar to persevere with his own dancing and he subsequently became world famous.[82] Pavlova herself danced in *Ajanta Frescoes* in Europe and the United States as well as in India during her second visit there in 1928-29. Another great Indian dancer, Rām Gopāl, "considered that *Ajanta Frescoes*, *Radha and Krishna* and *Hindu Wedding* marvellously captured the inner spirit of India and that without Pavlova there might not have been the great revival of Hindu dance, which now flourishes in India and all over the world."[83]

In the field of Russian music, the composer Aleksandr Skrjabin (1871-1915) was often preoccupied with occult concepts and plans of cosmic vastness. Among these were his plans for *Mystery*, a grandiose synaesthetic composition combining music, dancing, color, and odors (or scents) and involving two thousand performers. In Skrjabin's mind this was also to include a kind of ceremony set in an Indian temple; and Skrjabin, contemplating research, actually made inquiries in London in 1914 concerning fares to India and he even bought a sun helmet. But, though he seems to have mulled over this concept for about ten years, no essential progress was ever made.[84] Not too many years earlier, in 1897, Sergej Prokof'ev had written his first composition, the *Indian Gallop* in F Major, at the age of six. This was inspired by widely publicized reports of the famine in India as well as an outbreak of the plague in Bombay in 1896-98.[85]

In the previous chapter we mentioned the name of the nineteenth-century Russian painter, Vereshchagin, and his Indian paintings. In the Soviet period there were two painters who are perhaps most familiar in connection with India. One is Aleksandr Gerasimov (b. 1881). Though he is best known for his Russian landscapes, Gerasimov also has a series of Indian paintings that have attracted attention.[86] The other artist is Semen Chujkov (b. 1902) who also published a number of articles on his visits to India. Reproductions of some of Chujkov's Indian studies may be seen in various publications.[87]

If we consider the cinema an art form, then there are several items of interest with regard to Russia and India. Many Indian films have been shown in the Soviet Union and Soviet films are often seen in India.[88] But there have also been joint ventures of Soviet and Indian movie producers and the most interesting of these is the 1958 *Mosfil'm* production of Afanasij Nikitin's *Khozhdenie za tri morja* (see above, Chapter II, section 3). This was a joint Soviet-Indian production under the direction of Vasilij Pronin and Evgenij Andrikanis and the Indian director K. Abbas (music by A. Bisvas and B. Chajkovskij). The role of Nikitin was played by Oleg Strizhenov; amongst the Indian performers were the popular actress "Nargis" (F. Rashid) and the actor P. Kapur. One of the scenario writers, M. Smirnova, has a brief article on the making of the film, "Puteshestvie Afanasija Nikitina v Indiju", in *Kul'tura i zhizn'* (No. 1, 1957) and there are further details on the production in another article by B. Polevoj in *Ogonek* (No. 3, 1958).

7

On a somewhat lower level than most of the other literary works mentioned in this chapter are the Soviet novels of adventure, particularly those set in an oriental environment and, even more particularly, those set wholly or in part in India. There is, of course, no profusion of the latter, but the ones that are occasionally encountered belong, in a number of ways, to a tradition that goes back not only to certain nineteenth-century novels (such as those written by, for example, Rafail Zotov) but also to things like the anonymous *Gistorija o rossijskom matrose Vasilii Koriotskom* of an even earlier period. Novels of adventure, which frequently reflect certain actual personal experiences and adventures of the author, also quite often share some of the traditions of the autobiographical accounts of sea or land adventure (e.g., those of Vladimir Richiotti). Though the high tide of the paraliterary exotic adventure novel (especially in Western Europe) seems to have occurred during the first quarter of the present century,[89] I shall discuss here a more nearly contemporary specimen—Ivan Efremov's *Lezvie britvy* (1964).

Ivan Efremov (b. 1907) was trained in biology, geology, and paleontology. He traveled extensively on land and sea and is the author of numerous short stories and novels.[90] *Lezvie britvy* (which first appeared in periodical instalments), a lengthy work of four parts and over 600 pages, is hardly significant as literature; indeed, it reminds one, *mutatis mutandis*, of something like Chernyshevskij's *Chto delat'*?. This is especially noticeable in the Foreword where the author writes: "The aim of the novel is to show the special value that a knowledge of human psychology has at the present time in preparing a scientifically based education for people in a communist society". However, Efremov has managed to include in the latter half of the novel an amazing amount of factual matter concerning India. Not only does he mention those things that one usually finds in such works (gurus, suttee, karma, maya, Vedas, maharajahs, etc.) but he also touches upon, in the course of numerous lengthy dialogues and narrative passages, such matters as the Alexander Romance, the classics of Sanskrit literature (*Mahābhārata*, *Rāmāyaṇa*, *Śakuntalā*, *Vikramorvaśīya*, etc.), figures out of Hindu mythology (Urvaśī, Sītā, Draupadī, the Apsarase-s), and many other *recherché* details. He dwells upon the erotic element in Hinduism in considerable detail, with allusions to the sculptured figures at Khajurāho and Konārak, Vātsyāyana's *Kāmasūtra*, the *Anaṅga-Raṅga*, etc. There are many references to various divinities (especially female)—Kālī, Rati, Lakṣmī or Śrī—and he pays special attention to the Tantras (the "five M's", kuṇḍalinī, Śakti, etc.) and to the details of Haṭhayoga.

Efremov mentions a number of technical terms of Hindu philosophy and elaborates on the Indian religious dances, alluding, for example, to the "Bkharat Nat'ja" (i.e., *Bharata Nāṭya*) and even referring to the technical terms for various body positions and the dancer's girdle (*mekhalā*). In describing temple art, the author goes into further details concerning the different temple forms, the "vehicles" of the gods, the *dampatī* couples, etc. He includes many geographical names, ancient and modern, the Ajantā caves and wall-paintings, Mohenjo Daro, the streets, avenues, and other features of Calcutta and Bombay, and (in view of his professional background) even brings in *charnokit*—i.e., charnockite, a mineral named after Job Charnock, the founder of Calcutta. He also mentions many proper names, including those of Thomas Moore,

Marina Tsvetaeva, and—surprisingly—that "friend of the Indian people", Nikolaj Rerikh.

Though Efremov's *Lezvie britvy* is, as they say, a "mine of information", reminding us of the emphasis on "factography" so prevalent in Soviet fiction, as a novel it is insignificant and somewhat vulgar. But another side of Efremov, that of science fiction writer, may be seen in his *The Nebula of Andromeda* (1955), and Andrej Sinjavskij has some interesting comments on this novel in his article on Soviet science fiction.[91]

In other instances we find, as we do in the West, guru-types pictured in Soviet fiction as absurd and comical figures. A good example, although from a slightly earlier period, is the "Hindu guest" in Chapter XXXIII of Il'f and Petrov's *The Little Golden Calf* (1931). And, if we turn momentarily to emigré Russian literature, we encounter in the works of Vladimir Nabokov, for instance, occasional references to things Indian; but, as one might expect, such allusions are usually made for the sake of verbal puns of one kind or another. For example, in *Ada* there is a pun on, of all things, the name of the *Tripiṭaka* (Pali *Tipiṭaka*) or "three baskets" of Buddhist scriptures:

> "...I'll be back on the twenty-fifth. I have to deliver an address on the Psychology of Suicide"; and she had said, stressing, now that everything was *tripiṭaka* (safely packed), the exact kinship:..."[92]

As for themes and plots of ultimately Indian origin used in Russian prose fiction of the twentieth century, these have very likely, as in other modern literatures, become so altered, modified, supplemented, and attenuated over the ages in some cases until there is very little matter left that can be identified with any degree of certainty. In other cases the links and affiliations can be traced back to some point where we may see, at least, some connection with a story emanating from or otherwise connected with India. Let us take, for example, the story entitled *Otravlennyj sad* by Fedor Sologub (Teternikov) published in 1909 in the collection *Kniga ocharovanij.* This is a retelling of Nathaniel Hawthorne's "Rappacini's Daughter" which first appeared in 1844 and was later included in *Mosses from an Old Manse.*[93] The kernel of Hawthorne's story lies in a brief passage in Sir Thomas Browne which Hawthorne copied into his *American Notebook*, viz.,

> A story there passeth of an Indian King that sent unto Alexander a fair woman fed with Aconites and other poysons, with this intent, either by converse or copulation complexionally to destroy him.[94]

This suggestion of a plot was embellished by Hawthorne, re-embellished by Sologub (Dr. Rappacini becomes Dr. Botanik), and further embellished by Octavio Paz in his Spanish version.[95]

8

Of special interest are the monthly (and annual cumulative) listings, published in *The Indian National Bibliography* (Central Reference Library, Ministry of Education and Social Welfare, Calcutta), of the works of Russian literature which have been translated into the languages of India. A survey of some recent issues of the *Bibliography* shows a normal preponderance of prose works, most of which are translations made from earlier English versions rather than directly from the Russian. There is a wide chronological range, from Pushkin to the present; and, for the modern period, both emigré (or exiled) Russian writers are represented along with officially recognized Soviet authors. Thus there are translations of Solzhenitsyn's *Rakovyj korpus* (Hindi version: *Kainsar yard*, 1971) and *Arkhipelag Gulag* (Hindi version: *Gulag dvīp samūh*, 1975) as well as of Majakovskij's *Oblako v shtanakh* (Marathi version: *Pant ghaṭlelā dhāg*, 1971) and Sholokhov's *Tikhij Don* (Assamese version: *Dhire bai yay Dan*, 1970). Turgenev's *Otsy i deti* seems to be popular (Hindi version: *Pitā aur putra*, 1965; Malayalam version: *Pitākkanmārum putranmārum*, 1966), and, of course, the novels of Tolstoj (Punjabi version of *Vojna i mir: Jang te aman*, 1972; Assamese version of *Voskresenie*: *Nava jīvan*, 1972) and Dostoevskij (Telugu version of *The Idiot: Iḍiyaṭṭu*, 1966; Punjabi version: *Budhū*, 1971). There have been, over the years, many translations of Gor'kij's works, e.g., a fairly recent Bengali version of *Mat'* (*Ma*, 1972), and Chekhov's plays are well represented, e.g., a Malayalam version of *Vishnevyj sad* (*Cerittoṭṭam*, 1974).

Problems of translation are particularly acute in India and discussions of such problems frequently appear in books, articles, and symposia. Some years ago the Ministry of Scientific Research and Cultural Affairs published *The Art of Translation: A Sym-*

posium, containing articles by some twenty scholars and specialists.[96] References to Russian writers occur frequently in these articles. Thus V.S. Naravane disagrees with Nabokov's view that the "clumsiest literal translation is a thousand times more useful than the prettiest paraphrase". The same scholar also mentions the name of the late Harvard Russian specialist, Renato Poggioli, and quotes from his well-known essay, "The Added Artificer". The Hindi poet R. D. Sinhā mentions the intense activity of Soviet Russian scholars in the study of the languages of India and he suggests that the British and Americans follow the Soviet example. The Hindi journalist and author, S. Vātsyāyan, writes the following:

> Starting from the position that all expression is translation because it is the rendering of the unspoken...into speech...one could put forward the proposition that Silence is the ultimate literary art...And it would not indeed be an absurd statement; to the mystic all statements about art *except this* would appear questionable! Those who did not wish to go so far could yet assert that translation is *inherently* impossible because no word can fully substitute another: what is Flaubert's *mot juste* but the absolutely unique word, or the Confucian *ching ming* except the one and only name that a thing may be given? Or, for that matter, how far short of this position was the Imagists' belief that the perfect poem could have but one word (and that an untranslatable one, of course)?

Vātsyāyanjī (who sounds here remarkably like Jorge Luis Borges) perhaps did not know of Tjutchev's dictum, *Mysl' izrechennaja est' lozh'* ("a spoken thought is a lie") or of Gnedov's *Poèma kontsa* which consists of a blank page.

Though India may quite justifiably boast of having produced in Pāṇini the most renowned of ancient grammarians and, in his successors, some truly remarkable students of language and linguistic theory,[97] those newer tools in the study of language and literature now so popular in the West—such as semiotics and structuralism—have also been brought to bear by both Indian and European (including Soviet Russian) scholars on Sanskrit literary classics. For example, the Soviet Sanskrit scholar, A. Ja. Syrkin, the author of numerous studies of Sanskrit literature,[98] had an article in *Semiotica* (11:1, 1974, pp. 33-42) several years ago entitled "Notes on the *Kāma Sūtra*". Syrkin distinguishes the approach in Ovid's *Ars Amatoria* (which he calls "artistic didacticism") from the elaborate system of classification in the Hindu erotological work which he calls "scientific-didactic" (and, indeed, the *Kāma Sūtra* is a work of *madanatantra* or "sex science") and he compares Vātsyāyana's tendency to give full descriptions with that of modern science. Vātsyāyana, however, himself admits the special difficulties (and Syrkin quotes this passage): "To the degree that the effect of science extends, feeling in people is weak (*mandarasa*); when the wheel of pleasure (*rati*) begins to revolve, then there is no more science nor order (*kramaḥ*)". But Syrkin concludes his paper optimistically:

> Until now, the ancient Hindu study of *kāma* has naturally aroused the interest of modern readers and researchers largely owing to its content. Meanwhile, Vātsyāyana's descriptive method at times proves no less interesting for us than what he describes...We think that [Vātsyāyana], who examined this sphere of human behavior with a stringency, methodological insight, and profundity of observation remarkable for his time and subject, occupies a distinguished position in the history of scientific thought.

In another, more recent article in *Semiotica* (17:3, 1976, pp. 255-265), "The Emergence of Semiotics in India: Some Approaches to Understanding *Lakṣaṇa* in Hindu and Buddhist Philosophical Usages", the authors, A.M. Piatigorsky and D.B. Zilberman, discuss the quite different ways in which the sign (*lakṣaṇa*) is viewed in the Hindu and Buddhist traditions; they also claim that semiotics emerged in India in about the sixth century B.C. but disappeared under Hinduist, anti-Buddhist pressure. Their thesis seems to be quite valid:

> As for the problem of the concrete sign, we see that in Buddhism it has a form quite different from that of the *Gītā* and of the Brahmanic tradition. Krishna's preaching to Arjuna was exclusively an objective one and, as such, can be seen only from an outsider's point of view...[but] in the Hinayana Buddhist texts, the concrete sign is quite materialized and manifested in

> the term *anna* (Skt *ajña*) which literally means injunction for acquiring knowledge but implies the sign of seeing the Glorious Body of the Buddha (*sambhoga-kāya*) which appears before a meditator just a moment before his successful achievement of enlightenment.

Further evidence of this position may also be found, I presume, in the almost physical way in which the words *Om maṇi padme hūṃ* written on slips of paper are treated by Tibetan Buddhists (e.g., in prayer wheels).

In the various languages of modern India there are also numerous outlines and surveys of Russian literature. Some of these are quite bad—badly written and badly printed—but some are rather good. Amongst these latter there is, for example, K.N. Shukla's Hindi *History of Russian Literature* (*Rūsī sāhitya kā itihās*, Lucknow, 1963). This provides, in some 300 pages, a readable survey of Russian literature from the *Slovo o polku Igoreve* (*Igara ki sena ka gita*) to Aleksandr Fadeev.

It might be noted here, finally, that in January of 1970 a twenty-two-volume de luxe set of the new critical edition of the *Mahābhārata* was presented to the *Institut Vostokovedenija* in Leningrad by the Indian *chargé d'affaires* in the USSR. This elaborate edition, begun in 1927, was completed in 1966.[99]

9

So far as relations between the Republic of India (and Pakistan) and the Soviet Union are concerned, there has been a mass of both pro- and anti-Soviet books on this subject printed in India in recent years, and a number of these are in English. Very often the title of the book is indicative of the views held by the author or authors. For example, in *Shadow of the Bear*, edited by A. P. Jain,[100] there is a collection of short statements by various rather well-known Indians concerning the Indo-Soviet Treaty of 1971. Thus V. Shankar (former Defence Secretary to the Government of India) writes at the end of his statement ("A Carte Blanche for Infiltration by the USSR"):

> Judged in the light of the above and from the point of view of national interests, I am doubtful whether we had any justification for enthusing over the Treaty as we did immediately

after it was announced. Actually, that reminded me of an incident in English history. When Walpole, the peace-loving Prime Minister, was forced into a war, the people of England responded to that announcement by ringing their church bells. Walpole remarked: "They are ringing their church bells today; they would be wringing their hands tomorrow".

And A. G. Noorani, the Bombay political commentator, writes:

Mr. Thakur Das said that the Soviet Union helped us during the Chinese aggression. I am afraid there is overwhelming evidence, unrefuted by the Soviet Union, to show not only that the Soviet Union did not help us, but that it had advance knowledge of the Chinese invasion and that they approved of it before the event.

Pro-Soviet books published in India are apt to be extremely naive; if anyone doubts this, let him read, for instance, K. Neelkant's *Partners in Peace: A Study of Indo-Soviet Relations.*[101] The same may be said of certain articles which have found their way into collections of scholarly papers. I have in mind, for example, G.J. Ramarao's "Marxism: Indian History and Philosophy" in a *Festschrift* dedicated to the seventieth birthday of the German Indologist, Walter Ruben.[102] There is very good reason, of course, that such authors never refer to certain of Marx's own statements —e.g., whether we should have preferred India to have been conquered by Russians or Turks, or his statement that England, despite all her crimes, was in fact the instrument of history in India.[103]

CHAPTER VI

CONCLUSIONS

What I have done in the preceding chapters is, first, to describe briefly and chronologically the history of the West's discovery of and subsequent acquaintance with India—its peoples, religions, languages, and literatures; and, next, to point out some of the earliest references—often vague, crude or distorted—to things Indian in medieval and early modern Russian literature, as well as the earliest contacts between Russia and India, at the same time indicating the frequent occurrence of Byzantium as intermediary and noting the beginnings of Russian Indology. Thereafter I presented representative examples of the employment by both major and minor Russian prose writers and poets, from the eighteenth century to the present, of allusions to various aspects of India, accompanying this material with comments on such matters as the significance of the increased contacts between Russia and India, the growing scholarly interest, both in Russia and the West, in Indological and Sanskrit studies, and the special relevance of India for the romantic and neoromantic writers of Russia. The question now might well be asked, What is after all the value of such information and what conclusions may we reach in this regard?

We can state immediately that the influence on Russian literature, either over the centuries or at specific periods, of Indian thought in general and of the literature of India in particular cannot be called pervasive and cannot in any case rival those direct and seminal influences which emanated from Byzantium, Germany, France, England, and Italy. It would after all be absurd, carried away by a preoccupation with the heritage of India, for one to exaggerate the number, frequency, and significance of allusions to India in Russian and other European literatures, to find a Sanskrit prototype behind every other topos, and to treat hypotheses as certainties. But it would, I think, be equally absurd to ignore the presence—less than pervasive, to be sure, but nonetheless quite apparent and persistent—of such allusions to India as we have seen in the foregoing chapters. So far as the value of importance of these is concerned, there is, first, the general interest, on the part of both the specialist and the common reader, in the meaning and function of an allusion to some aspect of India in Russian literature (most often in poetry) as well as the desire—and occasionally the necessity—to explain and interpret it, whether this allusion be fairly clear and simple (as in the case of Gumilev's allusion to the Nala and Damayantī episode from the *Mahābhārata*) or somewhat more obscure (such as Khlebnikov's reference to the "black Vedas").

Then there is the philological interest, not only in those oft-noted affinities between Sanskrit and Russian but also in those words of Sanskrit, Pali, or Hindi origin encountered in Russian prose and poetry, either in Cyrillic transliteration (*nirvana*, *majja*, *amrita*, *mantra*, *agankara*, *purusha*, *tamas*, *tripitaka*, *mekhala*, *champak*, etc.) or—much more rarely—transliterated in Latin letters (as in Voloshin's *mulapracriti*). Interesting, too, are the names of deities and other figures out of Hindu mythology, as well as the frequent references to classical Sanskrit and Pali works and authors noted in the earlier chapters. In connection with these Indian lexical elements in Russian, a number of studies have been done of the use in Russian romantic verse of certain clusters of words either of actual oriental (including Indian) provenance or with marked exotic connotations; one such article was noted in Chapter V (note 4).

We have also noticed, in addition to frequent allusions to various cities, regions, and rivers of India as well as to specific architectural monuments, occasional references to historical events, such as Radishchev's note on the Black Hole of Calcutta and Tikhonov's allusion to the 1920 massacre at Amritsar. Quite apparent in this connection is the almost natural tendency of Russian writers—especially the Soviet poetasters—to utilize such allusions for polemical purposes. However, one generally meets with saner and more balanced views in the pre-revolutionary, non-Marxist Russian polemicists (witness Dobroljubov's comments on the Mutiny) than in the measured nonsense of their Soviet successors.

Generally speaking, the Western—especially romantic—poet or prose writer tends, for any given area of the Orient he is concerned with, to note, isolate, and emphasize extremes; and this, too, is quite natural. Any Western writer fortunate enough to have visited the Orient will have experienced those striking and occasionally shocking contrasts in wealth and poverty, beauty and ugliness, health and disease that are so apparent throughout the East (conversely, of course, the same holds true for an Oriental who visits the West); or, if the writer remains at home, relying on traditional tales and accounts by others of travels in the Orient, he will usually encounter these same contrasts, perhaps even more sharply drawn, in what he reads. Thus very many of the allusions to China in the literatures of the West may be grouped in relation to two poles: extremes of cruelty and of aesthetic sensitivity. In the case of Japan, a similar polarization is apparent; indeed, even in scholarly studies of Japanese culture one often finds discussions of such striking contrasts. As for India, it is (to some extent, because of its very size) the land *par excellence* of extremes: all of us can remember having seen at one time or another either pictures of, say, the Aga Khan's weight being matched in the scales by jewels or of people starving in the streets of Calcutta. These real extremes are clearly reflected, as we have seen, in Western literature. But perhaps they are most clearly contrasted in Russian literature: prior to the Revolution and beginning with the earliest texts it is "India the Rich" that is primary, while after the Revolution the Soviet Russian poets and prose writers (anticipated in this, as in other respects, by Belinskij and his followers) regularly dwell, with considerable relish, on "India the Poor".

But there are also other pairs of extremes that apply in the case of India—e.g., "India the Marvelous" and "India the Real" or—even more provocative—"India the Religious" and "India the Profane". I refer, for example, to what is an especially striking contrast for both the Western Christian and the Russian Communist, *viz.*, that between the Indian tradition of extreme religious devotion and asceticism on the one hand and the frank sensuality and sexuality that are so apparent in many aspects of Indic culture on the other. Again, while images related to Hindu or Buddhist religiosity bulk large in pre-revolutionary Russian literature, it is the more mundane and "real" side of India that is reflected in a good deal of Soviet literature. Although Russian writers traditionally avoid involvement with sexual matters (there are some notable exceptions, however), a visit to or an account of, say, the erotic sculptures at Konarak must make an especially piquant impression on the Russian writer, surrounded as he is by the quite different icons of orthodoxy, whether christian or Leninist. We have seen, I think, a good example of this appeal in the case of Efremov.

To my mind, two of the most interesting aspects of this or any similar study are the number and variety of classical Sanskrit and other Indian authors and works encountered in Russian literature, selections from which works have often been made available in translation by Russian writers; and the instances of either well-established literary affiliations between India and Russia or of cases when such affiliations are considered at least likely. A cosmopolitan outlook is always laudable and an acquaintance with the literatures of India is not only an enriching experience in itself; it provides the Russian poet with a wider range of metaphor and imagery, broadens both artist's and reader's horizons, and supplies the literary scholar and critic with further criteria in analyzing and evaluating those multifarious ways in which poets depict reality and verbalize their images.

As for the exploration, with reference to India and Russia, of literary sources, influences, and interconnections, although a great deal of work has, as we know, been done in the wider area of Indo-European comparative mythology, folklore, and thematics, this study has limited itself to the citation of several specific instances of the retelling of Indian tales and legends by Russian writers and a few instances when a theme of Indian origin turns up in the *byliny* and other items of Russian literature (such as the *Barlaam and Josaphat* apologue in Tolstoj's *Confession*). A number of other studies have been referred to which deal with research in this area (e.g., S. A. Fomichev's paper on the source of a Krylov fable, cited in Chapter II at note 46).

In the case of discussions of studies involved with tracing the influence of Indian—specifically Hindu and Buddhist—thought in the West, we are in a much more speculative area and one where there is an especial danger of exaggeration. Professor A. L. Basham writes in this regard:

> The influence of India on the rest of the world has always been most strongly felt in the fields of religion and philosophy, and this is still the case. It is easy to overemphasize the religious

> content of traditional Indian culture—at all times, but especially at the present time, the land has known a vigorous secular life. But from the time when Charles Wilkins first translated the *Bhagavad Gītā* into a European language, and Anquetil-Duperron the *Upaniṣads*, it has been the "spirituality" of India that has made the greatest impression on the Western observer.[1]

In this book, while avoiding extensive speculation, I have cited a number of instances when Russian poets and thinkers have dabbled in this or that area of Indian religious and mystical thought as well as an article or two exploring possible influence (e.g., of Buddhist thought in Dostoevskij). And of course there has been mention of some notable Russian scholarly studies in the field of Indian religious and philosophical speculation (e.g., Shcherbatskoj's *Buddhist Logic*).

In conclusion, I should like to quote the words of H.G. Rawlinson:

> As time goes on, the intellectual debt of Europe to India will be increasingly recognized, and a knowledge of her culture will be regarded as indispensable. "If I were to ask myself", said Max Müller, "from what literature we here in Europe, who have been nurtured almost exclusively on the thoughts of the Greeks and Romans, and one Semitic race, the Jewish, may draw that corrective which is most wanted in order to make our inner life more perfect, more universal, in fact, more human, I should point to India."[2]

Notes

CHAPTER I

1. For the background, see George Woodcock, *The Greeks in India* (London: Faber & Faber, 1966); and Donald Lach, *Asia in the Making of Europe* (Chicago: University of Chicago Press, 1965), vol. I, book 1, pp. 5-19. See also V. V. Bartol'd, *Istorija izuchenija Vostoka v Evrope i Rossii* (Leningrad, 1925).

2. Woodcock, pp. 17-20.

3. See B. Puri, *India in Classical Greek Writings* (Ahmedabad: New Order, 1963), p. 127.

4. Gold came to India, as it did to South Russia, from Siberia; see W. W. Tarn, *The Greeks in Bactria and India* (Cambridge: Cambridge University Press, 1966), p. 105 ff.

5. Cf. the Biblical Hebrew *Yewanim*. The rear curtain on the Indian stage (the Latin *siparium*) was called the *yavanikā*; see Tarn, p. 382 ff.

6. Woodcock, p. 20.

7. See J. Burnet, *Early Greek Philosophy* (London: A. & C. Black, 1975), p. 82, note 2.

8. Woodcock, p. 44.

9. See note 4. Tarn gives credit to an earlier work by the Russian historian M. I. Rostovtsev (Rostovtzeff), *The Social and Economic History of the Hellenistic World* (3. vols., 1941), and cites studies by the Russian scholar V. V. Bartol'd.

10. Woodcock, p. 68.

11. Indologists distinguish between *varṇa* ("color") as "class" and *jāti*, "caste"; our word "caste" comes from the Portuguese.

12. Tarn, p. 155.

13. On Nikitin, see below, Chapter II, section 3.

14. Robert Sencourt, *India in English Literature* (London, 1923), pp. 29-30.

15. See E. R. Curtius, *European Literature and the Latin Middle Ages*, transl. W. Trask (New York: Harper, 1963), pp. 160-161.

16. On the Slavic version of the *Topography*, see below, Chapter II, p. 25.

17. On the Slavic versions, see below, Chapter, II, p. 22.

18. See below, Chapter II, p. 23.

19. On the Old Russian *Aleksandrija*, see below, Chapter II, p. 20.

20. See V. Slessarev, *Prester John, a Popular Legend* (Minneapolis: University of Minnesota Press, 1961).

21. See below, Chapter II, p. 21.

22. See the Introduction in Franklin Edgerton, *The Panchatantra* (London: Allen & Unwin, 1965).

23. See, e.g., *Panchatantra*, transl. A. Adalis with preface by A. Syrkin (Moscow, 1962).

24. See L. W. Brown, *The Indian Christians of St. Thomas* (Cambridge: Cambridge University Press, 1956).

25. In Soviet prison-camp jargon the word *Indija* refers to a barracks housing prisoners who have lost all their clothes in card games; see M. Galler and H. Marquess, *Soviet Prison-Camp Speech: A Survivor's Glossary* (Madison: University of Wisconsin Press, 1972).

26. Sencourt, p. 89.

27. D. Chizhevskij, *History of Russian Literature from the Eleventh Century to the End of the Baroque* (The Hague: Mouton, 1960), p. 207.

28. For a detailed summary, country by country, see D. P. Singhal, *India and World Civilization* (East Lansing: Michigan State University Press, 1969).

29. On Bhartṛhari, see below, Chapter IV, p. 51.

30. Bartol'd, p. 180 ff. See also D. N. Druhe, *Russo-Indian Relations, 1466-1917* (New York: Vantage Press, 1970), p. 44 ff. On an earlier attempt to open trade relations with India, see Samuel Baron, "Vasilii Shorin: Seventeenth-Century Russian Merchant Extraordinary", in *Canadian Slavic Studies*, Winter, 1972, p. 524.

31. See A. Stein, *India and the Soviet Union* (Chicago: University of Chicago Press, 1969), Chapter I.

32. See A. Lobanov-Rostovsky, *Russia and Asia* (Ann Arbor: G. Wahl, 1951), pp. 100-101.

33. Lobanov-Rostovsky, pp. 124-125. See also the interesting comments on Russian Imperial General Staff plans for an invasion of India in M. Grulev, *Zapiski Generala-Evreja* (Paris, 1930), p. 113.

34. "Gentoo" (from the Portuguese *gentio*)=Hindu.

35. A Russian version of Wilkins' translation was published in 1788 by N. I. Novikov; see below, Chapter III, p. 35.

36. Karamzin published some scenes from the play, translated from Forster's German text, in 1972; see below, Chapter III, p. 35.

37. A. L. Willson, *A Mythical Image: The Ideal of India in German Romanticism* (Durham: Duke University Press, 1964), p. 69, note 12. Pushkin had a French version of Jones' translation of the *Śakuntalâ* in his library (*Sacontala, ou l'Anneau fatal*). On Tjutchev's Russian version of Goethe's "Sakontala", see below, Chapter IV, pp. 44-45.

38. Pushkin had in his library *Chefs d'oeuvre du théâtre indien* based upon Wilson's translations of Sanskrit works.

39. Willson, p. 210.

40. See F. Wilhelm and H. Rawlinson, "India and the Modern West", in *A Cultural History of India*, ed. A Basham (Oxford: Oxford University Press, 1975), pp. 473-474.

41. See R. K. Dasgupta, "G. S. Lebedev (1749-1817): The First Russian Indologist", in *Oxford Slavonic Papers*, vii (1957), p. 1 ff.

42. So Dasgupta as well as the *Bol'shaja Sovetskaja Èntsiklopedija.* See also J. C. Ghosh, *Bengali Literature* (Oxford: Oxford University Press, 1948), and Balwant Gargi, *Theatre in India* (New York: Theatre Arts, 1962) s.v. "Lebedeff".

43. See the material in *Russko-indijskie otnoshenija v XVIII v.* (Moscow,

1965). P. M. Kemp in his *Bharat-Rus* (Delhi: ISCUS, 1958) has a number of short chapters on Lebedev.

44. Full title in *Bibliografija Indii* (Moscow, 1976),≠10672. See also V. I. Kal'janov, "Sanskritologija", in *Aziatskij Muzej—Leningradskoe otdelenie Instituta Vostokovedenija AN SSSR* (Moscow, 1972), p. 235.

45. *Bibliografija Indii*, ≠2434. See also *Russko-Indijskie èkonomicheskie, nauchnye i kul'turnye svjazi v XIX v.* (Moscow, 1966), p. 117.

46. Available in English are Minaev's travel diaries: *Travels in and Diaries of India and Burma*, transl. H. Sanyal (Calcutta: Hind Printers, n.d.) with a biographical sketch by A. P. Barannikov. This contains reproductions of drawings by the Anglophile artist, Prince A. D. Saltykov, and of paintings of Indian scenes by Vereshchagin.

47. *Bibliografija Indii*,≠≠1020-1033. Shcherbatskoj's standard work in English translation, *Buddhist Logic*, is available in a two-volume paperback edition (Dover Publications, 1962).

48. See W. D. O'Flaherty, "Disregarded Scholars: A Survey of Russian Indology", in *South Asian Review*, July, 1972, pp. 289-304.

49. *Pratidanam: Indian, Iranian and Indo-European Studies Presented to F. B. J. Kuiper* (The Hague: Mouton, 1968).

50. *The Soviet Decipherment of the Indus Valley Script*, ed. A. Zide and K. Zvelibel (The Hague: Mouton, 1976). On Soviet Russian oriental studies, one should also consult R. Frye, "Oriental Studies in Russia", and W. Vucinich, "The Structure of Soviet Orientology", both in *Russia and Asia*, ed. W. Vucinich (Stanford: Hoover Institution Press, 1972). See also W. Laqueur, "The Shifting Line in Soviet Orientology", in *Problems of Communism*, No. 2, 1956, pp. 20-24.

CHAPTER II

1. See above, Chapter I, section 2, on the Byzantine versions.

2. See V. M. Istrin, *Ocherk istorii drevnerusskoj literatury domoskovskogo perioda* (Petrograd, 1922), p. 98 ff.

3. *Nagomudretsy* is a calque of the Greek *gymnosophistai*, "naked philosophers".

4. Dandamis in the classical sources.

5. *History of Russian Literature*, p. 94.

6. See C. A. van den Berk, "Wo entstand die sogenannte Serbische redaktion des Alexanderromans?", in *Slawistische Studien-Opera Slavica*, IV (Göttingen, Vandenhoeck & Ruprecht, 1963), pp. 343-358.

7. See A. S. Orlov, *Drevnjaja russkaja literatura* (M.-L., 1945), pp. 37-38. See also A. N. Robinson, "Indijskij uchenyj o 'Slove o polku Igoreve'. Osnovnye polozhenija doklada prof. S. K. Chatterdzhi na IV Mezhdunar. s"ezde slavistov v Moskve", in *Izvestija AN SSSR (lit. i jazyka)*, 19(1960), p. 243 ff.

8. Simply because this "Tale of the Indian Kingdom" was included with the *Slovo*, along with other secular matter, in the collection discovered by Count Musin-Pushkin in 1791. See also V. M. Istrin, *Skazanie ob indijskom tsarstve* (Moscow, 1893).

9. "In that India the rich/there was a young nobleman, Djuk Stepanovich".

10. Cf. the *tsarstvo indejskoe* incident in the *bylina* on Volkh Vseslav'evich and N. V. Vodovozov, "Bylina Kirsha Danilova o Volkhe i drevnie russko-indijskie otnoshenija", in *Trudy otdela drevnerusskoj literatury AN*, xiv (1958), pp. 212-216. See also Appendix II in P. M. Kemp, *Bharat-Rus*.

11. See S. F. Ol'denburg, "K voprosu ob istochnikakh Slova o dvenadtsati snakh Shakhaishi", in *Zhurnal Ministerstva narodnogo prosveshchenija*, St. P., No. II, 1892, pp. 135-140; and B. I. Kuznetsov, "Slovo o dvenadtsati snakh Shakhaishi", in *Trudy otdela drevnerusskoj literatury AN*, xxx (1976), pp. 272-278.

12. See Sh. I. Nutsubidze, *K proiskhozhdeniju grecheskogo romana "Varlaam i Ioasaf"* (Tbilisi, 1965), and K. Horalek, "Zu den christlichen Legenden orientalischer Herkunft", in *Das Heidnische und Christliche Slaventum= Annales Instituti Slavici*, II (Wiesbaden): Harrassowitz, 1969), p. 81 ff.

13. There is a Russian translation of the Arabic text in V. R. Rozen, *Povest' o Varlaame pustynnike i Ioasafe tsareviche indijskom* (M.-L., 1947).

14. In 1885 the *Obshchestvo ljubitelej drevnej pis'mennosti* published (No. LXXXIII) the text of the *Povest'*. See also A. Kirpichnikov, *Povest' o Varlaame i Ioasafe* (Khar'kov, 1876).

15. Chizhevskij, *History*, pp. 91-92. See also G. P. Fedotov, *The Russian Religious Mind* (New York: Harper, 1960), p. 136 ff.

16. See N. P. Popov, "Afanas' evskij izvod povesti o Varlaame i Ioasafe", in *Izvestija Otdelenija russkogo jazyka i slovesnosti AN SSSR*, xxxi (1926), pp. 189-230.

17. See G. A. Maloney, *Russian Hesychasm* (The Hague: Mounton, 1973), p. 200 ff.

18. Chizhevskij, *History*, p. 326.

19. See I. Franko, *Varlaam i Joasaf—starokhristianskij dukhovnij roman i jogo literaturna istorija* (L'viv, 1897). On Franko's translations of Indian literature, see below, Chapter IV, p. 62.

20. Tolstoy's version is quoted by R. Christian in *Tolstoy: A Critical Introduction* (Cambridge: Cambridge University Press, 1969), pp. 214-215.

21. See A. M. Remizov, *Povest' o dvukh zverjakh: Ikhnelat* (Paris: Opleshnik, 1950), p. 60.

22. For the original work, see Edgerton's *The Panchatantra*, pp. 23-76.

23. See below, Chapter III, p. 38, and Remizov, p. 60.

24. See note 21 above and Chizhevskij, *History*, p. 438.

25. Orlov, p. 24.

26. "As for the blasphemous fables concerning King Solomon and Kitovras, these are lies; there never was a Kitovras, but the Greek philosophers invented it".

27. Cf. I Kings, 6:7 (in Russian Bible, III Kings, 6:7). In Jewish folklore Solomon required the *shamir* (diamond); but in later versions the word refers to a tiny worm that does the cutting.

28. "Kitovras et Baš-Čelik", *Revue des Études Slaves*, 35(1958), p. 89 ff.

29. Ivanov's *Kitovras* may be found in *Cor Ardens* (Moscow: "Skorpion",

1911), p. 189. See also A. Mazon, "Le centaure de la légende vieux-russe de Salomon et Kitovras", *Revue des Études Slaves*, 8 (1927), pp. 42-62.

30. "The Voyage of Zosima to the Brahmans (The Voyage to the Terrestrial Paradise of the Blessed Anchorite Zosima".

31. Istrin, p. 102; Orlov, p. 191.

32. *History*, p. 28.

33. See J. S. Lur'e, "Une légende inconnue de Salomon et Kitovras dans un manuscrit du XVe siècle", *Revue des Études Slaves*, 43 (1964), pp. 10-11.

34. Published in 1886 by the *Obshchestvo ljubitelej drevnej pis'mennosti*, No. LXXXVI.

35. The illustrations were carefully studied by E. K. Redin in *Khristianskaja Topografija Koz'my Indikoplova po grecheskim i russkim spiskam* (Moscow, 1916). See also D. V. Ainalov, *The Hellenistic Origins of Byzantine Art*, transl. E. and S. Sobolevich (New Brunswick: Rutgers University Press, 1961), p. 25 ff.

36. Chizhevskij, *History*, p. 301.

37. *Russian Surnames* (Oxford: Oxford University Press, 1972), p. 130.

38. The best edition, with translation, notes, commentary, etc., is that of B. D. Grekov and V. P. Adrianova-Peretts (M. -L., 1948). Still a standard commentary is I. Minaev, *Staraja Indija. Zametki na Khozhenie Afanasija Nikitina* (St. P., 1882). See also the extensive listings on Nikitin in *Bibliografija Indii*, ≠1462 ff.

39. *History*, p. 209. But see the attempt by N. S. Trubetskoj, using Formalist methods, to "grasp the inner meaning of the work through its form" and to perceive the real artistic nature of the *Khozhenie* in "Afanasij Nikitin's *Journey Beyond the Three Seas* as a Work of Literature" in *Readings in Russian Poetics*, ed. L. Matejka and K. Pomorska (Cambridge: MIT Press, 1971), pp. 199-219. See also the article by Lowell Tillett, "The Soviet Popularization of Afanasii Nikitin's Trip to India: An Example of Planned Publishing in *Images of India* (New York: Humanities Press, 1971), pp. 172-191.

40. See R. Majumdar, H. Raychaudhury, and K. Datta, *An Advanced History of India* (London, 1951) for a high evaluation of Nikitin as a source (p. 363).

41. See the commentary by I. P. Petrushevskij and Grekov and Adrianova-Peretts, notes 124, 125.

42. See P. Winter-Wirz, "Die Fremdwörter in Afanasij Nikitins 'Reise über drei Meere' ", in *Zeitschrift für Slav. Phil.*, xxx (1962), pp. 86-113.

43. In Hindu mythology there was in fact a monkey-army and its king, *Sugriva*.

44. See A. N. Veselovskij, *Istoricheskaja poètika* (Leningrad, 1940), p. 508.

45. Cf. the Sheherazade episode in *A Thousand and One Nights*. See also V. Shklovskij, *O teorii prozy* (Moscow, 1929), pp. 83-84.

46. S. A. Fomichev in "Basnja Krylova 'Volk na Psarne' i ee literaturnyj istochnik" traces Krylov's fable back to the "Hunter and Wolf" apologue in the Syntipas collection; see *Sravnitel'noe izuchenie literatur* (Leningrad, 1976), pp. 31-34.

47. On Russian literature and Persia, see Aleksis Rannit, "Iran in Russian Poetry", *Slavic and East European Journal*, 3(1973), pp. 265-272.

48. Srinagar in Kashmir was known in Sanskrit as the "City of the Sun" (*Sūryanagara*).

49. See, e.g., Ju. Ovsjannikov, *Russkij lubok* (Moscow, 1962), Plate 14, showing Uruslan in the Indian Kingdom slaying the three-headed monster.

50. "Protopop Avvakum und das Phänomen der Selbstverbrennung" in *Slawistische Studien=Opera Slavica*, Band IV (Göttingen, 1963), pp. 531-536. See also D. I. Sapozhnikov, *Samosozhzhenie v russkom raskole* (Moscow, 1891).

51. See D. Zhukov and L. Pushkarev, *Russkie pisateli XVII veka* (Moscow, 1972), p. 238.

52. In later Russian poetry the Ganges is used in delimiting the extent of the Russian Empire—e.g., in Tjutchev, *Russkaja geografija* (1849): "From the Nile to the Neva, from the Elbe to China,/From the Volga to the Euphrates, from the Ganges to the Danube"; or it is contrasted with the Volga as in I. Dmitriev's *Volge* (1794): "Thou art more illustrious than the Ganges".

53. "Persia and India/and other states dare not oppose me".

54. *Besnovatye—Savva Grudtsyn i Solomonija* (Paris: Opleshnik, 1951), p. 30. See, incidentally, the interesting study by F. A. Rjazanovskij, *Demonologija v drevnerusskoj literature* (Moscow, 1915).

55. J. Fennell and A. Stokes, *Early Russian Literature* (Berkeley: University of California Press, 1974), p. 253.

56. Some scholars have found possible influence of the *Upaniṣads* in Plotinus; see E. Bréhier, *La philosophie de Plotin* (Paris, 1928), pp. 107-133.

57. *Op. cit.*, p. 27.

58. Quoted *Ibid.*, p. 276.

59. (New York: Harper & Row, 1960).

60. *Writings from the Philokalia on Prayer of the Heart*, transl. E. Kadloubovsky and G. Palmer (London: Faber & Faber, 1957).

61. *To Honor Roman Jakobson* (The Hague: Mouton, 1967), I, pp. 738-759.

62. *Pratidanam: Indian, Iranian and Indo-European Studies Presented to F. B. J. Kuiper* (The Hague: Mouton, 1968), pp. 108-120. See also Roman Jakobson's "Slavic Mythology" in *Funk & Wagnall's Standard Dictionary of Folklore, Myth and Legend* (New York: 1950), II, pp. 1025-1028.

63. See George Ivask, "Russian Modernist Poets and the Mystic Sectarians", in *Russian Modernism*, ed. G. Gibian and W. Tjalsma (Ithaca: Cornell University Press, 1976), p. 101.

CHAPTER III

1. S. N. Mukherjee, *Sir William Jones* (Cambridge: Cambridge University Press, 1968), pp. 5-6.

2. M. P. Conant, *The Oriental Tale in England in the Eighteenth Century* (New York: Columbia University Press, 1908), pp. 203-204.

3. *A Mythical Image: The Ideal of India in German Romanticism*, p. 23.

4. *L'Orient dans la littérature française* (Geneva: Slatkine reprints, 1970), p. 187.

5. For other names and details, see Klaus Städtke, *Die Entwicklung der russischen Erzählung*, 1800-1825 (Berlin: Akademie Verlag, 1971), pp. 26-29, 55-62. See also V. V. Sipovskij, *Ocherki iz istorii russkogo romana* (St. Petersburg, 1909), p. 653 ff. on L'vov.

6. Städtke, p. 56.

7. "The *Ta Hsüeh* or the Great Learning, containing the lofty Chinese philosophy". On China in 18th century Russian literature, see Barbara Maggs, *China in the Literature of Eighteenth-Century Russia* (doctoral dissertation, University of Illinois at Urbana-Champagne, 1973).

8. For other titles, see Sipovskij, p. 74. On Voltaire, see A. Debidour, "L'Indianisme de Voltaire", in *Revue de Littérature Comparée*, 4 (1924), pp. 26-40.

9. "They write from Persia that the Indian King has sent as a gift to our great Lord an elephant and many other things. It has been sent on by land from Shemakha to Astrakhan ' ".

10. See Druhe, *Russo-Indian Relations*, 1466-1917, p. 45.

11. Karamzin's scenes from *Śakuntalā* later appeared in *Panteon inostrannoj slovesnosti* in 1818.

12. "Nine years of travels and adventures of a Russian non-commissioned officer, now a collegiate assessor, in Bukhara, Khiva, Persia and India". See V. V. Pertsmakher, "Russkie morjaki v Indii v 60-x godakh XVIII v.", in *Strany i narody Vostoka* (Moscow, 1967), pp. 220-228.

13. Städtke, p. 56.

14. Full title in *Bibliografija Indii*, ≠3043.

15. On the sources of Lomonosov's knowledge of India, see G. Mühlpfordt, "Lomonosov und die Mitteldeutsche Aufklärung", in *Studien zur Geschichte der Russischen Literatur des* 18. *Jahrhunderts*, II (Berlin: Akademie Verlag, 1968), pp. 216-217.

16. There are further references to India in Kapnist's other versions of Horace. The Hydaspes is the Jhelum, a branch of the Indus.

17. See note 61 in Willson, *A Mythical Image*, p. 22.

18. This was described in detail in a supplement to *Moskovskie vedomosti* (No. 75, 1784, pp. 569-574): *Ob ovladenii bengal'skim nabobom Sudardzha Dovla anglijskoj Krepost'ju Vil'gel'm pri Kal'kutte v* 1756 *g.*

19. *Sochinenija Knjazja M. M. Shcherbatova* (St. Petersburg, 1896), I (*Politicheskie sochinenija*); see also A. A. Kizevetter, "Russkaja utopija XVIII stoletija", in *Istoricheskie ocherki* (Moscow, 1912), pp. 29-56.

20. See D. B. Neuenschwander, "Themes in Russian Utopian Fiction: A Study of the Utopian Works of M. M. Shcherbatov, A. Ulybashev, F. V. Bulgarin, and V. F. Odoevskij" (Syracuse University doctoral dissertation, 1974), p. 257.

21. See Paul Cornelius, *Languages in Seventeenth-and Early Eighteenth-Century Imaginary Voyages* (Geneva: Librarie Droz, 1965).

22. Richard Leonard, *A History of Russian Music* (New York: Macmillan, 1957), pp. 27-32.

CHAPTER IV

1. See Städtke, *Die Entwicklung der russischen Erzählung*, p. 55.

2. See E. Ja. Ljusternik, *Russko-Indijskie èkonomicheskie, nauchnye i kul'turnye svjazi v XIX v.* (Moscow, 1966).

3. See Index s.v. *Tūtīnāma* in Jan Rypka, *History of Iranian Literature* (Dordrecht: D. Reidel, 1968). A Russian translation of the *Tūtīnāma* by A. Balakin and P. Sukhotin was later published in Moscow: *Tuti-name* (Moscow, 1915).

4. Quoted in N. V. Riasanovsky, "Asia Through Russian Eyes", in *Russia and Asia*, ed. W. S. Vucinich (Stanford: Hoover Institution Press, 1972), pp. 11-12.

5. On Pogodin, see Riasanovsky, p. 13 ff. In 1834 Pogodin reviewed an annotated Sanskrit edition and translation of the *Mānavadharmaśāstra* (the code of laws attributed to Manu) prepared by A. Loiseleur DesLongchamps (*Bibliografija Indii*, ≠2432).

6. See J. H. Billington, *The Icon and the Axe* (New York: Vintage Books, 1970), p. 295.

7. See E. Feoktistov, "Magnitskij. Materialy dlja istorii prosveshchenija v Rossii", in *Russkij vestnik, June*, 1864, pp. 464-498; July, pp. 5-55.

8. In *Russkij vestnik*, November, 1879.

9. See above, Chapter I, section 5. The Japanese have recently published in three volumes a reprint of the short form of the Lexicon: *Sanskrit-Wörterbuch in kürzerer Fassung* (Tokyo: Meicho-Fukyu-Kai, 1976). A Sanskrit-English version of the dictionary is now being published by Motilal Banarsidass in Delhi.

10. See A. von Gronicka, *The Russian Image of Goethe* (Philadelphia: University of Pennsylvania Press, 1968), p. 157.

11. Lucien Petipa had earlier staged a *Sacountala* in Paris. See Natalia Roslavleva, *Era of the Russian Ballet* (New York: Dutton, 1966), p. 99 ff.

12. See Willson, *A Mythical Image*, p. 195, note 9.

13. See von Gronicka, p. 248. P. I. Chajkovskij at one time intended to write an opera entitled "Bog i bajaderka"; see *Polnoe sobranie sochinenij* (Moscow, 1974), XIV, p. 444.

14. Some twenty years later I. A. Kossovich produced a translation directly from Sanskrit. The Polish writer Antoni Lange (1863-1927), one of the first in Poland to popularize Indian philosophy and literature, later translated the Nala and Damayantī episode as well as the *Bhagavadgītā*.

15. The word shloka (*śloka*) as well as a number of other Sanskrit prosodical terms will be found in A. Kvatkovskij, *Poèticheskij slovar'* (Moscow, 1966).

16. On Zhukovskij as translator, see H. Eichstädt, *Zhukovskij als Uebersetzer*, in *Forum Slavicum*, 29 (München: W. Fink, 1970).

17. *Sobranie sochinenij v trekh tomakh* (Moscow, 1948), II, p. 690.

18. On Gumilev, see below, Chapter V, p. 76-77.

19. Batjushkov also has a *Son mogol'tsa* (1808) based on Lafontaine.

20. N. M. Lobikova, in the Introduction to her *Pushkin i Vostok* (Moscow, 1974), explains that "Vostok" in the title means "Blizhnij Vostok". See also I. Braginskij, "Zametki o zapadno-vostochnom sinteze v lirike Pushkina", in *Narody Azii i Afriki*, IV (1956), pp. 117-126.

21. On Chaadaev, see below, p. 62.

22. M. Volin, "Zagadka pushkinskogo proroka", in *Novoe Russkoe Slovo*, 7 Nov., 1976, p. 5.

23. See N. Izmajlov, "Iz istorii Pushkinskogo teksta. 'Anchar, drevo jada' ", in *Pushkin i ego sovremenniki*, xxxi-xxxii (1927), pp. 3-14; and D. Jakubovich *et al.*, "Zametki ob 'Anchare' ", in *Literaturnoe nasledstvo*, 16-18 (1934), pp. 869-884. On the Upas tree, see John L. Lowes, *The Road to Xanadu* (New York: Houghton Miflin, 1927), pp. 18-19 and notes.

24. *Polnoe sobranie sochinenij* (AN, 1938), X, p. 78. See also Ljusternik, p. 126, and the review of a Bengali translation of several of Pushkin's tales by the Indologist V. A. Novikova in *Russkaja literatura*, 2 (1958), pp. 209-210; and A. P. Barannikov, "Indijskie literaturovedy ob A. S. Pushkine", in *Izvestija AN SSSR* (*lit. i jazyka*), 8 (1949), pp. 229-233.

25. Ljusternik, p. 126.

26. "Sindy, Zund i sundary" in *Zhurnal ministerstva narodnogo prosveshchenija* (St. Petersburg, 1876), part 184, No. 3, pp. 1-49.

27. Text in *Poèty* 1820-1830-*kh godov* (Leningrad, 1972), I, p. 509. See below, Chapter V, p. 71, for a version by Brjusov of another poem from the Amaru collection.

28. *Ancient Indian Erotics and Erotic Literature* (Calcutta: Mukhopadhyay, 1959), p. 30.

29. See Willson, *The Mythical Image*, pp. 25-26 (note 17); also his note 3, p. 52, on the popularity of the pariah theme in Germany.

30. "Eternal Brahma, Lord of Glory,/Thou alone art the seed of all,/ And only thou alone art just.../Is it true that only Brahmins/And the rich and rajahs too/Were created by thee, O Lord,/Or are we and the beasts/Also the work of thy hands?"

31. Some of Bhartṛhari's verses had been translated in the seventeenth century by Abraham Roger (see above, Chapter I, p. 12). A German verse translation by Petrus Bohlen was published in 1835 and the poems were also available in French. In 1857 the *Biblioteka dlja chtenija* had published some of Bhartṛhari's poems, *Blizko i daleko*, translated from the Sanskrit by N. Berg.

32. *Bhartrihari: Poems*, transl. Barbara Stoler Miller (New York: Columbia University Press, 1967), p. 97.

33. In V. I. Majkov, *Sochinenija i perevody* (St. Petersburg, 1867), pp. 169-170. See above, Chapter III, p. 35.

34. Städtke, p. 59. The story was republished in *Sobranie obraztsovykh russkikh sochinenij i perevodov v proze* (St. Petersburg, 1816).

35. See the long list of other translated tales and fables in *Bibliografija Indii*, ≠ ≠9394-9407.

36. See M. Lemke, *Nikolaevskie zhandarmy i literatura* 1826-1855 *gg.* (St. Petersburg, 1908), p. 305. But associations between Christ and Kṛṣṇa are frequently encountered; see, e.g., M. P. Dragomanov, *Notes on the Slavic Religio-Ethical Legends*, transl. E. W. Count (Bloomington: Indiana University Russian and East European Series, 1961), 23, p. 104.

37. *Polnoe sobranie sochinenij* (Moscow, 1949), XVI, pp. 542, 546.

38. *Ibid.*, p. 396.

39. The former work was also reviewed in 1854 by the orientalist Osip Senkovskij ("Baron Brambeus") in *Biblioteka dlja chtenija.* Chernyshevskij's

reviews appeared in *Otechestvennye zapiski*, No. 7, 1853, and No. 3, 1854.

40. See N. Bogoslavskij, *N. G. Chernyshevskij* (Moscow, 1955), p. 227.

41. See V. Nabokov, *Dar*, Chapter IV. The *Om* formula is used appropriately by Zabolotskij in his *Rubruk v Mongolii*; see below Chapter V, p. 83.

42. On the Russian reaction to the events of 1857 in India, see N. V. Riasanovsky, "Asia Through Russian Eyes", p. 14.

43. See M. D. Beljaev, ed., *Ostrovskij: novye materialy* (Leningrad, 1924), p. 161. The text of the comedy is printed in full. Jacolliot's translation was *La Devadassi* (*Bayadère*). *Comédie en quatre parties* (*attribuée a Parasourama*) *traduite du tamoul par L. Jacolliot* (Paris, 1868).

44. Jacolliot was a French civil official in India.

45. See P. Birjukov, "Tolstoj i vostok", in *Novyj Vostok*, No. 6, 1924, pp. 392-402; and Derk Bodde, *Tolstoy and China* (New York: Johnson Reprint Corp., 1967).

46. See above, Chapter II, p. 23, on Tolstoj's use of a Barlaam and Josaphat apologue in his *Ispoved'*.

47. This and the following passages are from the first section of Chapter I in *Le roman russe*.

48. The word "nihilism" is usually associated with Turgenev and his novel, *Fathers and Sons* (1862); but Nikolaj Nadezhdin had used the word in 1829 (*Vestnik Evropy*, nos. 1 & 2). Still earlier, the word "nihiliste" was listed in Mercier's *Néologie* of 1801 and it was first used in French in 1796.

49. It is also used by Sir Isaiah Berlin as an epigraph to his essay, *The Hedgehog and the Fox*.

50. Translated by S. E. Roberts in *Essays in Russian Literature*: *The Conservative View: Leontiev, Rozanov, Shestov* (Athens: Ohio University Press, 1968), p. 245.

51. See È. E. Zajdenshnur, "Fol'klor narodov Vostoka i tvorchestvo L. N. Tolstogo", in *Sovetskoe Vostokovedenie*, No. 6, 1958.

52. In Buddhist literature an *avadāna* is an edifying tale exemplifying the workings of *karma*.

53. La Salle: Open Court, 1973.

54. Tolstoj's Russian version may be found in *Polnoe sobranie sochinenij* (Moscow-Leningrad, 1954), XXXI, pp. 47-57.

55. Tolstoj, as we know, had a special interest in the philosophy of Schopenhauer; on Schopenhauer and India, see Willson, *The Mythical Image*, p. 124 ff.

56. See L. Grossman, *Balzac and Dostoevsky*, transl. Lena Karpov (Ann Arbor: Ardis, 1973), pp. 36-39.

57. "Buddhistic Elements in 'The Idiot' " in *Studia Slavica* (Budapest), xviii (1972), pp. 77-84.

58. An article in the Bombay *Times of India* (14 Jan., 1904) describes the popularity in India of Tolstoj, Chekhov, and Vereshchagin. See also P. Barannikov, "Indija chitaet Chekhova", in *Sovremennyj Vostok*, No. 1, 1960, p. 47.

59. *Letters of Anton Chekhov*, ed. A. Yarmolinsky (New York: Viking Press, 1973), pp. 169-170. See also the article by M. Kolodochko, "Chekhov v Indii i Kitae", in *Don*, No. 10, 1959, pp. 152-155.

60. *Letters of Anton Chekhov*, p. 345. Khavkin died in Paris. See M. Popovskij, *Sud'ba doktora Khavkina* (Moscow, 1963).

61. But there is a reference in *Oblomov* (Part I, vi) to the story of Eruslan Lazarevich; see above, Chapter II, p. 28.

62. It is interesting, by the way, that Goncharov's *Oblomov* exerted considerable influence in Japan—witness the novel *Ukigumo* (Drifting Cloud) by Futabatei Shimei (1864-1909). See S. Shigeki, "The Influence of Russian Literature in Japan", in *Japan Quarterly*, July-September, 1960, pp. 343-349.

63. Quoted in Milton Ehre, *Oblomov and His Creator* (Princeton: Princeton University Press, 1973), pp. 143-144.

64. *Polnoe sobranie sochinenij* (St. Petersburg, 1901), XI, pp. 3-115.

65. Franko's version of the Manu tale is based on Albert Höfer's *Indische Gedichte in deutschen Nachbildungen* (Leipzig, 1844); the Sunda and Upasunda episode is based on Franz Bopp's *Ardschuna's Reise zu Indra's Himmel, nebst anderen Episoden des Maha-Bharata* (Berlin, 1868).

66. All the above translations may be found in volume 14 of *Tvori* (New York: Knigospilka, 1959).

67. Quoted in *Peter Yakovlevich Chaadayev: Philosophical Letters and Apology of a Madman*, transl. M. Zeldin (Knoxville: University of Tennessee Press, 1969), p. 171.

68. Published in *Izvestija Imp. AN po otdeleniju russkogo jazyka* (St. Petersburg, 1855), vol. 4, No. 3, col. 385-429. See also Nicholas Lossky, *History of Russian Philosophy* (New York: International Universities Press, 1951), p. 31.

69. See N. Berdjaev, *Aleksej Stepanovich Khomjakov* (Moscow: Mamontov, 1912), *passim.*

70. I have used the second edition of the English translation by Nathalie Duddington (London: Constable, 1898).

71. Paris: Aubier, 1952, p. 277, in the chapter, "Le bouddhisme et la pensée européenne".

72. N. Roslavleva, *Era of the Russian Ballet*, pp. 146-147.

73. See the autobiography, *Chaliapin*, transl. and ed. N. Froud and J. Hanley (New York: Stein & Day, 1967), p. 304.

74. Ljusternik, p. 156. In his bibliography Ljusternik cites a work which I have not seen: *Indija v proizvedenijakh khudozhnikov* (Moscow, 1955).

75. See above, Chapter I, at note 46.

76. Ljusternik, pp. 126-127, and Kemp, *Bharat-Rus*, pp. 211-213.

77. See T. V. Venttsel', *Tsyganskij jazyk* (Moscow, 1964).

78. See A. P. Barannikov, "Tsyganskie èlementy v russkom vorovskom argo", in *Jazyk i literatura*, 7 (1931), pp. 139-158.

CHAPTER V

1. Russian and English texts in *Fifty Soviet Poets* (Progress Publishers, Moscow, 1969), pp. 20-21.

2. *Zivilizationsflucht und literarische Wunschraüme: Der exotische Roman im ersten Viertel des 20. Jahrhunderts* (Stuttgart: Metzler, 1975), p. 103.

3. E.g., in Vjacheslav Ivanov's *Po zvezdam.* But A. F. Koni, in his *Pamjati Turgeneva*, taking the phrase to mean "This is also you", applies it to Turgenev, able as a writer to put himself in another's place.

4. *Champak* (i.e., the champac tree) is of Sanskrit origin. "Parmi les expressions dont ils [i.e., the romantic poets] ont enrichi le vocabulaire poétique se distinguent des mots designant des objets charactéristiques du milieu oriental...Sous maints aspects, le goût de l'exotisme coincide avec celui de l'orientalisme", Hana Jechova, "Le rôle des exotismes dans le style de la poésie romantique chez les Slaves", in *Revue des Études Slaves*, 49 (1973), p. 204.

5. *Three Mughal Poets* (Cambridge: Harvard University Press, 1961), p. 228. See also my article on *The Russian Ghazal* in *Symposium* (Syracuse University), Winter, 1964, pp. 342-351.

6. Mir Taqi's "Advice to Bad Poets" had been translated earlier into Russian from the French version of Garcin de Tassy (Paris, 1826), The Russian translation appeared in *Atenej*, No. 13, 1829.

7. Marc Slonim, *Russian Theater* (New York: Collier Books, 1962), p. 238. See also Ju. Golovashenko, *Rezhisserskoe iskusstvo Tairova* (Moscow, 1970), for many references to *Sakuntala*.

8. Cf. the reference to Tagore in Sosnora's poem *Rozy*, below, p. 84. See also the numerous entries on Tagore in the *Bibliografija Indii*. Ju. Baltrushajtis, another Russian symbolist poet, translated (from English) excerpts from Tagore's *Gītāñjali*; in *Zavety*, No. 11 (1913), pp. 116-120.

9. *The Crescent Moon* (London: Macmillan, 1913), p. 18. The Bengali title was *Kena Madhur*.

10. This and other legends are given by Professor Arthur Ryder in his Introduction to Kālidāsa, *Shakuntala and Other Writings* (New York: Dutton, 1959).

11. See K. Mochulsky, *Andrej Belyj: His Life and Works*, transl. N. Szavalitz (Ann Arbor: Ardis, 1977), p. 19.

12. It is interesting that Vinogradov utilizes these passages to illustrate *avtorizovannaja literaturnaja rech'* and the *dialekticheskoe rassloenie* of the auctorial "I" in *O teorii khudozhestvennoj rechi* (Moscow, 1971), pp. 194-195.

13. Quoted in Samuel Cioran, *The Apocalyptic Symbolism of Andrej Belyj* (The Hague: Mouton, 1973), p. 61 ff.

14. See above, Chapter IV, p. 71.

15. Published in *Vesy*, No. 1, 1907; the Latin title refers to the positions (333) of sexual intercourse.

16. I use with permission the translation of Vladimir Markov and Merrill Sparks in *Modern Russian Poetry* (New York: Bobbs-Merrill, 1967), p. 143.

17. See the examples quoted by D. Chizhevskij in his *History of Russian Literature*, p. 254.

18. See M. Maline, *Nicolas Gumilev: Poète et critique acméiste* (Bruxelles: Académie Royale de Belgique, 1964), p. 109 ff.

19. The "thee" is Anna Akhmatova.

20. The full translation may be found in *Stikhotvorenija* (Moscow, 1958), pp. 126-127.

21. Quoted in S. Ghose, *The Later Poems of Tagore* (Calcutta: Asia Publishing House, 1961), p. 77.

22. Mandel'shtam, because of his Jewish background, might have known of the Jews of Southern India (in Cochin); see Sylvain Lévi, "Quelques docu-

ments nouveaux sur les Juifs du Sud de l'Inde", in *Memorial Sylvain Lévi* (Paris: Hartmann, 1937), pp. 364-368.

23. *Sobranie sochinenij*, ed. G. Struve and B. Filippov (Washington: Inter-Language Literary Associates, 1964), I, p. 158.

24. *Hope Against Hope*, transl. Max Hayward (New York: Atheneum, 1976), pp. 247-248.

25. E. g., in the *Slovar' inostrannykh slov*, s.v. "Buddizm": "...igraet reaktsionnuju rol', sposobstvuja poraboshcheniju trudjashchikhsja èkspluatatorskimi klassami".

26. I refer to Herzen's "Buddhism in Science". See Sydney Monas" Introduction in *Complete Poetry of Osip Emilevich Mandelstam*, transl. Burton Raffel and Alla Burago (Albany: State University of New York Press, 1973), pp. 2-3.

27. *Sobranie sochinenij*, I, p. 155 ff.

28. *Ibid.*, p. 159.

29. The *Bibliografija Indii* has three entries citing Gorodetskij's translations of the works of the Hindustani writer, Wafa.

30. See Ju. Loshchits and V. Turbin, "Tema Vostoka v tvorchestve V. Khlebnikova", in *Narody Azii i Afriki*, 4 (1966), pp. 147-160.

31. See S. Mirsky, *Der Orient im Werk Velimir Chlebnikovs* (München: Otto Sagner, 1975), p. 34.

32. The full text of the poem, together with an English translation, may be found in *Modern Russian Poetry*, pp. 335-337.

33. Mirsky, pp. 31-32.

34. *Ibid.*, p. 83.

35. The poems are listed in *Stikhi* 1936-1959, ed. G. Struve and B. Filippov (Ann Arbor: University of Michigan Press, 1961), p. 284.

36. In *Russische Romantik* (Köln: Böhlau Verlag, 1975), p. 34 ff.

37. *Stikhi* 1936-1959, pp. 185-186. On *champak*, see above, note 4.

38. *Sobranie sochinenij* (M., 1973), vol. I, p. 22. Tanjore is the site of a large temple of Śiva.

39. I. L. Grinberg in his *Tvorchestvo Nikolaja Tikhonova* (M., 1972) lauds *Indijskij son* as an example of Tikhonov's *faktichnost'* and *dokumental'nost'* (p. 57).

40. *Sobranie sochinenij*, vol. II, pp. 219-222. The poem was dedicated to Marietta Shaginjan.

41. Grinberg, p. 44. See also Gleb Struve, *Russian Literature Under Lenin and Stalin*, 1917-1953 (Norman: University of Oklahoma Press, 1971), p. 74.

42. *Through the Glass of Russian Literature*, ed. E. Simmons (New York: Columbia University Press, 1961), pp. 170-171.

43. See Grinberg, p. 438 ff.

44. *Sobranie sochinenij*, IV, p. 214.

45. *Nikolaj Zabolotskij*: *Stikhotvorenija*, ed. G. Struve and B. Filippov (Washington: Inter-Language Literary Associates, 1965), p. 185.

46. *Ibid.*, p. 239 ff. William of Rubruck was a thirteenth-century explorer in Mongolia.

47. Sofronov has a series of articles, "Indijskie zapiski iz putevogo dnevnika pisatelja", in several issues of *Ogonek* for 1955, as well as a number of

other prefaces and introductions to collections of modern Indian writers.

48. L. N. Tolstoj, *Polnoe sobranie sochinenij* (M., 1956), XXXVII, pp. 259-272.

49. See A. Sergeenko, "Perepiska Tolstogo s M. K. Gandhi", in *Literaturnoe nasledstvo*, 37-38, 1939.

50. Alexandre Kaplan, *Gandhi et Tolstoi* (Nancy: Stuquert, 1949); K. Nag, *Tolstoy and Gandhi* (Patna, 1950); Martin Green, *Tolstoy and Gandhi* (New York, 1983). See also R. Fülöp-Miller, *Lenin and Gandhi* (London: Putnam, 1930).

51. See D. J. Richards, "Comprehending the Beauty of the World: Bunin's Philosophy of Travel", *Slavic and East European Review*, Oct., 1974, pp. 514-532.

52. See S. Kryzytski, *The Works of Ivan Bunin* (The Hague: Mouton, 1971), pp. 130-133.

53. *Revue de Littérature comparée*, 2 (1922), p. 7.

54. Quoted in D. I. Belkin, "Vostok v dorevoljutsionnom tvorchestve M. Gor'kogo", in *M. Gor'kij i literatury zarubezhnogo Vostoka* (M., 1968), pp. 261, 263.

55. See N. A. Vishnevskaja, "Indologicheskie knigi v lichnoj biblioteke M. Gor'kogo", in *M. Gor'kij i literatury...*' pp. 293 (note 1) and 302.

56. See the brief items of correspondence between Gor'kij and B. R. Cama in *Perepiska A. M. Gor'kogo s zarubezhnymi literatorami* (M., 1960), p. 221 ff.

57. *Novyj mir*, 9 (1932), p. 15 ff.

58. See A. A. Bobrova, "Dejatel'nost' Vostochnoj Kollegii 'Vsemirnoj literatury' pod rukovodstvom M. Gor'kogo", in *M. Gor'kij i literatury...*' p. 281 ff.

59. See B. Ishboldin, "The Eurasian Movement", in *Russian Review*, Spring, 1946, pp. 64-73; and Otto Boss, *Die Lehre der Eurasier* (Wiesbaden, 1961).

60. T. Burrow, *The Sanskrit Language* (London: Faber & Faber, 1955), pp. 18, 20, 79-80.

61. Vasmer cites the Sanskrit word s.v. *medved'* but erroneously gives it as *madhuvád.*

62. In *Selected Writings. I: Phonological Studies* (The Hague: Mouton, 1962), pp. 144-201.

63. *To Honor Roman Jakobson* (The Hague: Mouton, 1967), I, pp. 770-784.

64. *The Meaning of the Creative Act*, transl. Donald Lowrie (New York: Collier, 1962), pp. 149-150, 278-279.

65. "Torgovye puti mezhdu Indieju i Kitaem" in *Izvestija Imp. russkogo geogr. obshchestva* (St. Petersburg, 1869), vol. 5, no. 1, pp. 16-19.

66. *Ethics: Origin and Development*, transl. L. Friedland and J. Piroshnikoff (New York: Dial Press, 1934), p. 310.

67. "Osnovy Vedaizma" in *Sobranie sochinenij* (St. Petersburg, 1911), VI, pp. 172-232.

68. One of his paintings, *Slavjane na Dnepre* (1905), is reproduced in *Paintings from the Russian Museum Collection* (Leningrad: Aurora Publi-

cations, 1975). Others may be found in *The Nicholas Roerich Exhibition* with an introduction, catalog of paintings, and bibliography by C. Brinton (New York: Redfield-Kendrick-Odell, 1972). His paintings are in many of the museums of Europe and the United States as well as India (Tagore Collection, Balpur).

69. See his *Altai-Himalaya: A Travel Diary* (New York: Stokes, 1929). I have also seen Rerikh's *Tverdynja plamennaja* (New York: *Vsemirnaja liga kul'tury*, n.d.).

70. See W. S. Vucinich, "The Structure of Soviet Orientology", in *Russia and Asia*, ed. W. S. Vucinich (Stanford: Hoover Institution Press, 1972), pp. 130-131.

71. Another similar article by Rerikh appeared in *The Journal of Oriental Research* (Madras), No. 27, 1957-58, pp. 48-77. A number of articles by Rer ikh in English which had originally appeared in various scholarly journals were reprinted in the Soviet Union in 1967 by the Academy of Sciences—*Ju. N. Rerikh: Izbrannye trudy.*

72. *Jesus in Indian Paintings* (Madras, 1975), p. 97.

73. See, e.g., È. P. Zinner, "Kipling-Poèt v Rossii", in *Sravnitel'noe izuchenie literatur* (Leningrad, 1976), pp. 309-314.

74. *Rudyard Kipling*, ed. John Gross (London: Weidenfeld & Nicholson, 1972), p. 11.

75. *Rudyard Kipling to Rider Haggard*, ed. Morton Cohen (London: Hutchinson, 1965), p. 136. Kipling also felt that the troubles in Russia were due to the machinations of Jews (p. 110).

76. See *For Freedom of Imagination*, transl. L. Tikos and M. Peppard (New York: Holt, Rinehart & Winston, 1971), pp. 187-188.

77. Quoted in *A Voice from the Chorus*, transl. K. Fitzlyon and M. Hayward (New York: Farrar, Straus & Giroux, 1976), p. 211.

78. É. Kuznetsov, "O khudozhnike Pakhomove i ego illjustratsijakh k skazke Kiplinga", in *R. Kipling. Koshka, g͡uljajushchaja sama po sebe* (Leningrad, 1971), p. 17.

79. G. Lukács, *Studies in European Realism* (New York: Grosset & Dunlap, 1964), p. 258.

80. See *A Sentimental Journey*, transl. Richard Sheldon (Ithaca: Cornell University Press, 1970), p. 153 and note 44.

81. See the detailed description of the first night in Richard Buckle, *Nijinsky* (New York: Avon, 1975), pp. 234-237.

82. He died in 1977 at age 76; see the obituary notice in *The New York Times*, 27 Sept., 1977, p. 40.

83. Oleg Kerensky in *Anna Pavlova* (New York: Dutton, 1973), p. 96.

84. Richard Leonard, *A History of Russian Music* (New York: Macmillan, 1957), p. 217. See also the literature cited in Billington, *The Icon and the Axe*, p. 483, note 34.

85. Claude Samuel, *Prokofiev* (New York: Vienna House, 1971), p. 21.

86. See "Indijskie ètjudy Aleksandra Gerasimova" in *Iskusstvo*, No. 5, 1954, pp. 27-31.

87. E.g., in an album with a foreword by L. Zinger in *Sovetskij khudozh-*

nik, No. 5, 1958; one of Chujkov's Indian paintings is included in *Paintings from the Russian Museum Collection*, ≠163.

88. See the entries in the *Bibliografija Indii*, ≠ ≠ 9909-9959.

89. See Wolfgang Reif, *op. cit.* Reif refers mainly to German and other West European writers.

90. See the bibliographical note by V. Ivanov, pp. 738-742, in Efremov's collection, *Velikaja duga* (Moscow, 1956).

91. *For Freedom of Imagination*, p. 17 ff.

92. *Ada*, Part Three, 1 (last paragraph).

93. See Andreas Leitner, *Die Erzählungen Fedor Sologubs* (München: Otto Sagner, 1976), p. 96. I also refer to this connection in *Defamiliarization in Language and Literature* (Syracuse: Syracuse University Press, 1977), pp. 150-151.

94. *Pseudodoxia Epidemica*, Book VII, Chapter xviii, quoted in Randall Stewart, ed., *The American Notebooks by Nathaniel Hawthorne* (New Haven: Yale University Press, 1932), p. lxxi.

95. See R. C. Sterne, "Hawthorne Transformed: Octavio Paz's *La hija de Rapaccini*", in *Comparative Literature Studies*, September, 1976, p. 230 ff. Sterne refers to Paz's quoting from the *Sūtra Prajñāpāramitā* in his *El Arco y La Lira*. See also Joe Davis, "The Myth of the Garden: N. Hawthorne's 'Rappaccini's Daughter' ", in *Studies in the Literary Imagination*, 1-2 (1968-69), p. 3 ff.

96. New Delhi, 1962.

97. See *A Reader on the Sanskrit Grammarians*, ed. J. F. Staal (Cambridge: MIT Press, 1972).

98. E.g., "K probleme sinestizii v indijskoj èstetike" in *Problemy teorii literatury i èstetiki v stranakh Vostoka* (Moscow, 1964); and "O komicheskom v drevneindijskoj obramlennoj povesti" in *Simpozium po teoreticheskim problemam vostochnykh literatur* (Moscow, 1966).

99. V. I. Kal'janov, "Sanskritologija", in *Aziatskij Muzej—Leningradskoe Otdelenie Instituta Vostokovedenija AN SSSR* (Moscow, 1972), p. 257.

100. New Delhi: P. K. Deo, 1971.

101. Delhi: Vikas Publishing House, 1972.

102. *Neue Indienkunde*, ed. H. Krüger (Berlin: Akademie-Verlag, 1970), pp. 331-343.

103. The passages in Marx are quoted in full in Isaiah Berlin, *Marx* (New York: Oxford University Press, 1959), pp. 186-187.

CHAPTER VI

1. *A Cultural History of India* (Oxford: Oxford University Press, 1975), p. 496.

2. *Modern India and the West*, ed. L. S. S. O'Malley (Oxford: Oxford University Press, 1941), p. 566.

SELECTED BIBLIOGRAPHY

Works in English, French, and German:

Baron, Samuel, "Vasilii Shorin: Seventeenth-Century Russian Merchant Extraordinary", *Canadian Slavic Studies*, Winter, 1972, pp. 503-548.

Basham, A., ed., *A Cultural History of India* (Oxford: Oxford University Press, 1975).

Basham, A., *The Wonder That Was India* (New York: Hawthorn Books, 1963).

Brown, L., *The Indian Christians of St. Thomas* (Cambridge: Cambridge University Press, 1956).

Burrow, T., *The Sanskrit Language* (London: Faber & Faber, 1955).

Chizhevskij, D., *History of Russian Literature from the Eleventh Century to the End of the Baroque* (The Hague: Mouton, 1960).

Christian, R., *Tolstoy: A Critical Introduction* (Cambridge: Cambridge University Press, 1969).

Dasgupta, R., "G. S. Lebedev (1749-1817): The First Russian Indologist", *Oxford Slavonic Papers*, vii (1957), p. 1 ff.

Dragomanov, M., *Notes on the Slavic Religio-Ethical Legends* (Bloomington: Indiana University Russian and East European Series, 23, 1961).

Druhe, D., *Russo-Indian Relations* 1466-1917 (New York: Vantage Press, 1970).

Edgerton, F., *The Panchatantra* (London: Allen & Unwin, 1965).

Fedotov, G., *The Russian Religious Mind* (New York: Harper, 1960).

Galler, M. and Marquess, H., *Soviet Prison-Camp Speech: A Survivor's Glossary* (Madison: University of Wisconsin Press, 1972).

Ghose, S., *The Later Poems of Tagore* (Calcutta: Asia Publishing House, 1961).

Ghosh, J., *Bengali Literature* (Oxford: Oxford University Press, 1948).

Green, M., *Tolstoy and Gandhi* (New York, 1983).

Gronicka, A. von, *The Russian Image of Goethe* (Philadelphia: University of Pennsylvania Press, 1968).

Horalek, K., "Zu den christlichen Legenden orientalischer Herkunft", *Das Heidnische und Christliche Slaventun=Annales Instituti Slavici* (Wiesbaden), ii (1969), p. 81 ff. *Images of India* (New York: Humanities Press, 1971).

Ishboldin, B., "The Eurasian Movement", *Russian Review*, Spring, 1946, pp. 64-73.

Jechova, H, "Le rôle des exotismes dans le style de la poésie romantique chez les Slaves", *Revue des Études Slaves*, 49 (1973), pp. 203-215.

Kaplan, A., *Gandhi et Tolstoi* (Nancy: Stuquert, 1949).

Kemp, P., *Bharat-Rus* (Delhi: ISCUS, 1958).

Kirk, I., "Buddhistic Elements in 'The Idiot' ", *Studia Slavica* (Budapest), xviii (1972), pp. 77-84.

Lach, D., *Asia in the Making of Europe*, 2 vols. (Chicago: University of Chicago Press, 1965-1977).

Laqueur, W., "The Shifting Line in Soviet Orientology", *Problems of Communism*, 2 (1956), pp. 20-24.

Lobanov-Rostovsky, A., *Russia and Asia* (Ann Arbor: G. Wahl, 1951).

Lur'e, J., "Une légende inconnue de Salomon et Kitovras dans un manuscrit du XVe siècle", *Revue des Études Slaves*, 43 (1964), pp. 10-11.

Maloney, G., *Russian Hesychasm* (The Hague: Mouton, 1973).

Martino, P., *L'Orient dans la littérature française* (Geneva: Slatkine Reprints, 1970).

Miller, B., transl., *Bhartrihari: Poems* (New York: Columbia University Press, 1967).

Minaev, I., *Travels in and Diaries of India and Burma* (Calcutta: Hind Printers, n.d.).

Mirsky, S., *Der Orient im Werk Velimir Chlebnikovs* (München: Otto Sagner, 1975).

Mukherjee, S., *Sir William Jones* (Cambridge: Cambridge University Press, 1968).

O'Flaherty, W., "Disregarded Scholars: A Survey of Russian Indology", *South Asian Review*, July, 1972, pp. 289-304.

Nag, K., *Tolstoy and Gandhi* (Patna, 1950).

O'Malley, L., ed., *Modern India and the West* (Oxford: Oxford University Press, 1941).

Pratidanam: Indian, Iranian and Indo-European Studies Presented to F. B. J. Kuiper (The Hague: Mouton, 1961).

Rannit, A., "Iran in Russian Poetry", *Slavic and East European Journal*, 3 (1973), pp. 265-272.

Reif. W., *Zivilizationsflucht und literarische Wunschraüme: Der exotische Roman im ersten Viertel des 20. Jahrhunderts* (Stuttgart: Metzler, 1975).

Russell, R. and Islam, K., *Three Mughal Poets* (Cambridge: Harvard University Press, 1961).

Rypka, J., *History of Iranian Literature* (Dordrecht: D. Reidel, 1968).

Sencourt, R., *India in English Literature* (London, 1923).

Singhal, D., *India and World Civilization* (East Lansing: Michigan State University Press, 1969).

Slessarev, V., *Prester John: A Popular Legend* (Minneapolis: University of Minnesota Press, 1961).

Städtke, K., *Die Entwicklung der russischen Erzählung*, 1800-1825 (Berlin: Akademie Verlag, 1971).

Stcherbatsky [Shcherbatskoj], F., *Buddhist Logic* (New York: Dover Publications, 1962).

Stein, A., *India and the Soviet Union* (Chicago: University of Chicago Press, 1969).

To Honor Roman Jakobson (The Hague: Mouton, 1967).

Vogüé, M. de, *Le roman russe* (Paris, 1896).

Vucinich, W., ed., *Russia and Asia* (Stanford: Hoover Institution Press, Stanford University, 1972).

Willson, A., *A Mythical Image: The Ideal of India in German Romanticism* (Durham: Duke University Press, 1964).

Winter-Wirz, P., "Die Fremdwörter in Afanasij Nikitins 'Reise über drei Meere' ", *Zeitschrift für Slav. Phil.*, xxx (1962), pp. 86-113.

Zide, A. and Zvelibel, K., ed., *The Soviet Decipherment of the Indus Valley Script* (The Hague: Mouton, 1976).

Works in Russian:

Aziatskij Muzej—Leningradskoe otdelenie Instituta Vostokovedenija AN SSSR (Moscow, 1972).

Barannikov, A., "Tsyganskie èlementy v russkom vorovskom argo", *Jazyk i literatura*, 7 (1931), pp. 139-158.

Bartol'd, V., *Istorija izuchenija Vostoka v Evrope i Rossii* (Leningrad, 1925).

Beljaev, M., ed., *Ostrovskij: novye materialy* (Leningrad, 1924).

Bibliografija Indii (Moscow, 1976).

Birjukov, P., "Tolstoj i Vostok", *Novyj Vostok*, 6 (1924), pp. 392-402.

Braginskij, I., "Zametki o zapadno-vostochnom sinteze v lirike Pushkina", *Narody Azii i Afriki*, iv (1956), pp. 117-126.

Franko, I., *Varlaam i Joasaf—starokhristianskij dukhovnij roman i jogo literaturna istorija* (L'viv, 1897).

Gor'kij, M., i literatury zarubezhnogo Vostoka (Moscow, 1968).

Grekov, B. and Adrianova-Peretts, V., ed., *Topografija Khristianskaja* (Moscow-Leningrad, 1948).

Istrin, V., *Ocherk istorii drevnerusskoj literatury domoskovskogo perioda* (St. Petersburg, 1922).

———, *Skazanie ob indijskom tsarstve* (Moscow, 1893).

Jakubovich, D. and others, "Zametki ob 'Anchare' ", *Literaturnoe nasledstvo* 16-18 (1934), pp. 869-884.

Kirpichnikov, A., *Povest' o Varlaame i Ioasafe* (Khar'kov, 1876).

Kolodechko, M., "Chekhov v Indii i Kitae", *Don*, 10 (1959), pp. 152-155.

Lobikova, N., *Pushkin i Vostok* (Moscow, 1974).

Loshchits, Ju. and Turbin, V., "Tema Vostoka v tvorchestve V. Khlebnikova", *Narody Azii i Afriki*, 4 (1966), pp. 147-160.

Ljusternik, E., *Russko-indijskie èkonomicheskie, nauchnye i kul'turnye svjazi v XIX v.* (Moscow, 1966).

Minaev, I., *Staraja Indija: Zametki na Khozhenie Afanasija Nikitina* (St. Petersburg, 1882).

Nutsubidze, Sh., *K proiskhozhdeniju grecheskogo romana "Varlaam i Ioasaf"* (Tbilisi, 1956).

Orlov, A., *Drevnjaja russkaja literatura* (Moscow-Leningrad, 1945)

Popovskij, M., *Sud'ba Doktora Khavkina* (Moscow, 1963).

Problemy teorii literatury i èstetiki v stranakh Vostoka (Moscow, 1964).

Rozen, V., *Povest' o Varlaame pustynnike i Ioasafe tsareviche indijskom* (Moscow-Leningrad, 1947).

Russko-Indijskie otnoshenija v XVIII v. (Moscow, 1965).

Sipovskij, V., *Ocherki iz istorii russkogo romana* (St. Petersburg, 1909).

Simpozium po teoreticheskim problemam vostochnykh literatur (Moscow, 1966).

Sravnitel'noe izuchenie literatur (Leningrad, 1976).

Venttsel', T., *Tsyganskij jazyk* (Moscow, 1964).

Veselovskij, A., *Istoricheskaja poètika* (Leningrad, 1940).

Vodovozov, N., "Bylina Kirsha Danilova o Volkhe i drevnie russko-indijskie otnoshenija", *Trudy otdela drevnerusskoj literatury AN SSSR*, xiv (1958), pp. 212-216.

Zajdenshnur, È., "Fol'klor narodov Vostoka i tvorchestvo L. N. Tolstogo", *Sovetskoe Vostokovedenie*, 6 (1958).

INDEX